An Alban Institute Publication

Letting go

transforming

Congregations for Ministry

Roy D. Phillips

foreword by Michael Cowan

To my companion Patricia Harmon

and my children

Joseph, Luke, Lisa, and Nicolas

for all they have helped me learn
about the paradox of letting go into togetherness

CONTENTS

FOREWORD

Roy Phillips is uneasy. He worries about the spiritual vitality of today's established congregations. For this reader, the most telling (and amusing) symbol of the congregational malaise at which Phillips takes aim is the "Pigeon Control Committee." Drawing on more than thirty years' experience as a senior pastor, he describes in these pages a process by which congregations may grow out of a concern for maintaining the ecclesiastical organization and into a transformational orientation.

That growth, he believes, requires four shifts:

- *From membership*, in which congregants understand themselves as recipients of spiritual care from professional providers, *to ministry*, in which they carefully discern their gifts and the responsibilities to which these gifts correspond;
- *From entitlement*, in which congregants remain members because they are given standing influence over some piece of the congregation's life, *to mission*, in which they become mindful of calls to service both inside and outside the congregation;
- *From education*, in which congregants are consumers of a curriculum designed and delivered by others, *to spiritual development*, in which they interrupt the frenetic "doing" of contemporary life in order to attend to the movement of the spirit in their lives and the response the spirit asks of them;
- *From toleration*, in which congregants politely allow otherness but keep it at arms length, *to engagement*, in which they embrace diversity as a source of ongoing spiritual transformation.

Pastors and lay leaders approaching this book with practical hopes, needs, and questions will not be disappointed. The chapters devoted to the four critical shifts in congregational mentality and behavior include both real stories about how the congregation Phillips pastored for nearly three decades was prompted by the spirit to make those shifts, and practical strategies for leading a congregation through them.

Embedded within these four "why and how-to" chapters are pointed questions for reflection, intended to encourage readers to connect their life experience with the text's stories and explanations. The four main chapters are punctuated by interludes of poetry, dialogue, and practical wisdom, which introduce a meditative dimension to the reading.

We must not let the practical, pastoral nature of this book blind us to its prophetic probing of the status quo, however. I find two significant and timely critiques, one cultural and one theological, woven into the heart of the book. Culturally, Phillips challenges both the consumerist and self-actualizing individualisms of contemporary Western cultures, and the individualistic quasi-spiritualities to which such individualisms give rise—spiritualities that propose one's ultimate calling is either to "own a piece of the rock" or to "be all you can be."

Against this cultural juggernaut, he invokes the image of congregations and their members as communal or relational beings. As such, they are under continual obligation not only to discern and respond to their own true interests, but to be in solidarity with others and to be prepared to challenge the larger world of which they are a part in the name of the common good. This is the theme of "communities of call."

Theologically, Phillips contrasts two religious visions on which congregational life can be founded, a two-world or a one-world ecclesiology. The two-world view of classical Western theism explicitly or implicitly discounts the importance of events within nature and history by its steady privileging of a better world yet to come. In sharp contrast, the one-world view—to be found, for example, in the philosophical theology of Whitehead, Wieman, Meland, Loomer, Cobb, Lee and others—locates the activity of God squarely within nature and history. Phillips notes, rightly, that a one-world natural and historical theology resonates profoundly with the Jewish religious vision. As I followed this dimension of the text, I remembered the opening words of one of my teachers, Bernard Loomer, in a course on process/relational theology: "Ladies and gentleman, do not lose sight of the fact that in the theological world we are about to enter, there is no supernatural escape hatch." Roy Phillips makes it plain that his hope and motivation for congregational transformation are deeply rooted in the incarnational theological intuition that reality is not bifurcated into natural and supernatural realms, that the world of the transforming God—historical, natural, spiritual—is one. Perhaps because I write these words on Yom Kippur, I find myself paraphrasing the classic words proclaimed in the synagogue this morning: "Hear, O Israel, the Lord our God—and the world God made—are one."

Many authors leave the impression that their writing springs full blown from their own minds. In engaging moments of spiritual and intellectual autobiography, Roy Phillips traces his evolving understanding of congregational transformation to their sources, identifying not only specific events in a long career of innovative ministerial leadership within the Unitarian tradition, but also his ongoing immersion in the intellectual and religious currents of American transcendentalism and process/relational philosophical theology. By doing so, he illuminates not only his own but America's development of an authentic alternative to the classic European neo-orthodox renditions of the gospel.

Conversation happens when two or more partners seek the truth on a subject of mutual interest. Because this shared seeking of truth worth living is incompatible with attempts to control its process and outcome, Gadamer warns us that "a genuine conversation is never the one we wanted to conduct." This thoughtful and valuable book is a partner, waiting to converse with anyone interested in engaging with a wise and committed practitioner on the critical subject of the vitality of America's religious congregations as Christian communities of faith enter their third millennium. May it lead you into a conversation you did not expect!

> Michael A. Cowan
> Professor, Institute for Ministry
> Loyola University New Orleans

ACKNOWLEDGMENTS

This book on energizing people for ministry begins with a sense of gratitude for "the mighty cloud of witnesses" who have energized me in my ministry. The list goes on and on, but a few must be mentioned by name because they have opened large doors for me into new worlds: Joseph Barth and Duncan Littlefair, my principal mentors in parish ministry, both of whom were early students of Henry Nelson Wieman; Barbara Johnson, who opened me to the power of paradox in my living, preaching, and in parish life; William Dean, who led me back into the power of the American empiricist, process/relational school of religious thought; my colleague Barry Andrews who pointed me to Emerson scholar David Robinson, whose work, in turn, showed me the spiritual importance of the New England transcendentalists and the American Renaissance; Lawrence Palmieri Peers, whose lively sense of so many of these things has encouraged me and shown how many resources there are; Michael Cowan, social scientist and theologian who teaches the possibility of living one's theology in speaking and listening to one another.

Many lay leaders in congregations I have served have brought home to me again and again the remarkable ways experiential education, spiritual deepening, organizational structure, and the practice of ministry all belong together. Among these lay leaders, I especially want to thank Laurel Hallman (who has long since become a colleague), Carolyn Gallagher, Michael Miner, Maura Williams, Michael Patton, and Linda Giesen.

The work of two others has shown the way into a richer practice of ministry. Jean Trumbauer in her lively, meticulous work shows how to help people discern and direct their gifts for day-by-day ministry in congregations and in the world. Mary Ann Jens taught me what she has taught many—the basic skills needed for reflecting with others in a spiritually deepening way on the practice of ministry.

My colleague Ruppert Lovely rough-and-tumbles and challenges my every new idea, disapproves of my optimism, and profoundly supports me at every turn. Our friendship over the decades has been a constant source of energy for my ministry.

Beth Ann Gaede, the editor of this book, has been the skilled midwife of its birthing by cajoling and encouraging it into being all along the way.

PREFACE

This book grows out of a deepening uneasiness about the quality of life in the established congregations of our day. My unease participates in a widespread cultural mood and attaches to traditional, mainline, and liberal congregations. But these pages are written in hope. The widening dissatisfaction with existing congregational realities is a sure sign to me that we have begun trusting that something else–something better–is possible. We couldn't notice how bad it is until we first came to sense the possibility of a better way. An old millennium closes; a new millennium opens. Hope arises.

Over more than three decades I served as the key ordained leader of just two congregations. They were both generally seen as "healthy" and "successful." My first ministry, lasting fewer than four years, was in a small Wisconsin congregation that was being reawakened through the efforts of a skilled and hopeful few after a long, slow time of diminishment. My other settlement, lasting more than 27 years, was as lead minister of a large, expanding congregation, Unity Church-Unitarian in Minnesota's capital city. Beginning near the close of the terribly painful Vietnam War, that second ministry helped to stir a pioneering sense of new beginning within the congregation, a broadening out past the conventional limits of denominational identity, and a renewal in program, administration, spirit, and ministry.

The challenges encountered in the course of those two ministries drew me, during much of the second half of the 20th century, into lively engagement in the religious conversation in North America. As a practitioner in ministry, I was moved to converse with others and to read what thoughtful people were writing. I was hoping for a better understanding. But more, I was seeking savvy, practical skills to help me engage with the more difficult human and institutional challenges that inevitably emerged in my work.

I began to join with others within and beyond my own religious community in exploring innovations toward more creative and satisfying congregational life. As a result, great changes stirred within the Minnesota congregation I was serving. I know how fortunate I was to be located in that religious community whose deep, pervasive health enabled it to endure and be strengthened by the strains of change that came as it allowed itself to be a pilot-project congregation.

I was also eager to absorb whatever theologically informed thinking was going on regarding life in congregations. Looking at things theologically energizes me by giving my experience its richest possible grounding.

I was drawn to write down some of my discoveries and my hunches and send them off into the world in various formats. That was a way, as a parish minister, I could share with others what I was learning and also have those learnings tested in a wider community dialogue.

Originating in congregational reality and always returning to it, my perspective as practitioner in a parish provided what seems to me the best imaginable place for reading the vital signs of the remarkable, unique, sometimes disturbing, but always intriguing form of religious community we know as *congregation.*

Through all this—leading, ministering, observing, reading, trying new things, reflecting, writing, conversing—I kept approaching something I needed to learn, not only in my work, but in my living. It would glimmer on for me, I would almost get there, and then it would fade away. This is still a struggle and a challenge for me: learning to let go; letting go, even when I am exercising responsibility—indeed, letting go as a powerfully effective way of being responsible. This is the quest embedded in the whole span of this book, both in its four main chapters and in its "Letting Go . . ." interludes.

One can understand this quest into the capacity to let go as a *practical* consideration: developing the skills needed to lead others by getting out of the way of those one leads. It can also be seen as a *spiritual* concern: Do I trust? How far do I trust? Do I have faith that there are powers at work in and among lives and events that are creative, sustaining, transformational? And it can be seen as a *theological* consideration: Is God operating in the situations and events of my world? Can I confidently "let go and let God" in my relationships with others, in my leadership, and in my work, even as I apply myself and my skills vigorously? In each of the sections of this book, these practical, spiritual, and theological considerations will be raised, both as part of my story and as reflective questions for the reader's use.

The questions along the way are intended to distract the reader from too much linearity of thought. The hope here is that these questions will invite readers and groups of readers into a personalized and localized experience of the book's themes as a way of increasing their capacity to discern issues that might be stirring in their own congregations.

In the 1940s, through the generosity of Susan Minns, a fund was established at King's Chapel and at First and Second Church in Boston to afford Unitarian ministers the opportunity to share their perspectives on religious matters. The honor of being named the Minns Lecturer for 1995 brought me to the Graduate Theological Union in Berkeley, California, where I spoke to a small group of clergy, laity, faculty, and students, most of whom were associated with the Starr King School for the Ministry, in whose Fireside Room the lectures were first delivered and enriched. Those lectures were made into a book by the Minnesota congregation in honor of the first 25 years of our time together. Since its publication, I have been invited north, east, south, and west as speaker, preacher, and seminar and workshop leader for clergy and lay leadership gatherings in congregations, clusters of congregations, and theological schools. The conversations that have occurred in these widely scattered places have expanded my perspective as well as demonstrated conclusively to me that something new is trying to emerge in congregational life.

This new book folds these rich experiences and conversations into the thesis of the original book. It deepens the theological reflection and seeks to move the conversation into wider circles.

I have encountered a vast number of people, scattered in various places, who are working in a territory of the spirit that knows nothing of the old denominational boundaries. Countering community-destroying forces of the times, they are reawakening the deep and mystical sense of community and creativity that has characterized the religious vision at its best. That vision is of "life in the spirit." It is shared ministry. For moments, at least, it is a flash-forward into the "new heaven and new earth" imagined, predicted, preached, and promoted from of old.

INTERLUDE 1

Can any of you by worrying add a single hour to your span of life?

If then you are not able to do so small a thing as that, why do you worry about the rest?

Consider the lilies, how they grow: they neither toil nor spin; yet I tell you, even Solomon in all his glory was not clothed like one of these.

But if God so clothes the grass of the field, which is alive today and tomorrow is thrown into the oven, how much more will he clothe you—you of little faith!

(Luke 12:25-28)

Sitting silently, doing nothing,
Spring comes, and the grass grows by itself.

—A Zen saying

The "Letting Go" Interludes

Every transition begins with an ending. As life goes on and we encounter anything that changes—and everything does—we are faced with yet another ending that requires us once again to let go. New things come only after we let go of former things. But letting go of what is familiar is not most people's favorite thing.

Letting go requires a sense deep down that there is that which can be trusted. That sense does not come to most of us once and for all. It needs to be remembered and recovered again and again in every new phase of our life.

At times this "good not our own" is palpable to us and we readily feel we can rely upon it. We know it has been and is at work in the world inspiring springtime grasses and flowers and all manner of creatures great and small, including persons, to come into being, to blossom, and to bear fruit. There are other times, though, when all that is obvious to us is that we have energies to exert, wills to assert, decisions to make, and things to do so that existing structures won't fall apart and so that new realities can come into being.

Putting together our power with power not our own is perhaps life's greatest challenge. To assert oneself and then to let go. To connect with others and to let go. To hold on to what we cherish and to let go. Every parent has to learn this, as does every teacher, leader, friend, lover, family member, and every person who works for organizational transformation and community change—everyone who has a ministry.

The interludes of this book offer reflections, thoughts of others, and exercises intended to help us work our own way through the issues encountered in letting go.

CHAPTER 1

From Membership to Ministry

I found the cartoon posted on a corridor wall in a congregation in Dallas. It was titled "New Member's Worst Nightmare." An elderly man with a long, flowing beard is speaking to a young couple new to the church. The couple looks at a huge bulletin board listing all the congregation's committees. At the top is emblazoned: "Our Committees Need You!"

The old man says, "Most people are on nine or ten committees, but since you're new, I'm sure people will understand if you only join six or seven to start." The best part of the cartoon is the list of committees themselves: Finance Committee, Investment Committee, Board of Trustees–yes. But the list goes on . . . Thermostat Control Committee, Committee for More Comfortable Pews, Committee for the Promotion of Committees, Plant Watering Committee, Pigeon Control Committee.[1] The cartoon is a good one. It makes me wince. And it makes us laugh–or not–because it's so close to the truth.

How many committees or other work groups are there in your congregation? In which of these have you served?

Those people who have been thinking and writing about congregational administration over the years have given us some theoretical underpinnings for encouraging committee involvement. Early in my ministry I learned one theorist's step-by-step breakdown of what any and every congregation should be prepared to do for newcomers.

First, *invite people*. When they arrive, *welcome*

What was your first experience with your congregation? How long was it before you were noticed? When did you feel most taken seriously? What happened to give you that feeling?

them. Next, *orient them* to what's available for them in the congregation. Then, *help them to join*. Finally, *assimilate them into the congregation's life.*

Books, seminars, and many consultants present strategies by which these membership considerations (invite, welcome, orient, join, assimilate) can be carried out. These sources sound the warning, however, that congregation after congregation does a fine job with the first four, then falls down on the fifth. New people join but never are assimilated. They come in with enthusiasm but drift off because they haven't become deeply engaged in the congregation's life. This is identified as *the problem of membership retention.*

The almost universally recommended solution to this problem is to get each new person involved in carrying out the congregation's work as early in membership as possible. Most of the time this means finding committees on which they can serve. Thus, the cartoon suggests that newcomers join "six or seven to start."

I have a problem with this approach. Our congregations have problems because of it. I'm encouraging us to listen more carefully to ourselves as we think, "She is new, and we want her to stay with our congregation. To keep her with us, we must keep her engaged, must give her a way to feel important here. The best way to do that is to provide her with something to do." There's something inappropriate in this automatic reaction, and this book will suggest that we go in a different direction.

Fortunately (or unfortunately), we know there is always plenty that needs doing. So it seems natural enough for us to turn attention from the newcomer directly to the tasks needed to maintain the congregation and its activities: managing finances, maintaining the building, teaching classes, greeting visitors, or raising money. Then we ask ourselves, "Which of these might interest her enough to get her to say 'yes'? What tasks do we have that will keep her with us?"

Beneath this conventional approach to newcomers is an underlying assumption: she needs to feel needed, and the best way for that to happen is for us to give her a congregational job to do. But maybe that assumption isn't valid. Maybe she won't be able to find what she really needs from her religious community by serving a two-year stint on a pigeon control committee, a religious education committee, or a vestry. Even if *she* supposes that it's what she needs, maybe congregational committee work isn't the best thing her congregation can give her. Such a task might just be more busyness to feed her busyness habit. Carl George, a widely read theoretician of a small-group method of promoting church growth among evangelical Christians, has written:

How do you know you are needed in your congregation? In your family? By your friends? At work? In your community?

> Some denominations, like the Presbyterians, Lutherans, and Episcopalians, have become captive to the upper middle class. How does a church keep these often materialistic, high-power people interested and involved? One solution is to offer them a seat on the church board, or after that's filled, to place them on a significant committee, giving them veto-making authority in order to meet their power needs. In some smaller churches, up to half the adult membership is involved in one of these groups.[2]

Perhaps this evangelical leader's words raise our defenses with their mention of class, values, and power. It may bother us to read his sweeping, even accusatory, dismissal of what has become conventional wisdom about new-member retention.

Do we detect our own defensive response to his words? Can we move past our immediate response? Can we let ourselves reconsider what we simply assume is the norm?

I do not think of myself as an evangelical, but I find myself agreeing with Carl George's observations.

What is the "class" makeup of your congregation? What tells you that? Do you consider yourself in that group?

People come to our congregations looking for bread. We tend to give them the stones of busyness and pseudo-power. Sometimes they return the favor by holding onto that power for dear life, squeezing the stone for blood in all the petty, power-driven ways so familiar in congregations. They turn the attention and expend the resources of religious community on the wrong concerns, and they damage their own and other people's spirits in the process. All the while, by holding onto institutional power, they keep everything the same and run down everybody's morale. Subtly and not so subtly, they keep newcomers from really coming in, and they assure that the congregation will not be characterized by much light, clarity, vibrancy, or magnanimity. We should try for something better.

What They Come Hoping For

In his book *Effective Church Leadership*, congregational consultant Kennon Callahan wrote about the condition of the church in the latter years of the 20th century. He wrote some powerful and disturbing things. His experience in a lively United Methodist congregation and in working as a consultant with many other congregations reflected what I too have seen in my work primarily among liberal congregations:

> People come to a church longing for, yearning for, hoping for ... [a] sense of roots, place, belonging, sharing, and caring. People come to a church in our time with a search for community, not committee.
>
> We make the mistake of assuming that, by putting people on a committee, they will develop ownership for the objectives of the church. People are not looking for ownership of objectives. ... They are looking for the profound depths of community. ... Jesus said, "I must be about my Father's business." He did not say "busyness."[3]

In this unsettling passage Callahan goes on to say that for a while, because of their strong desire for community, some of those people will look past "the silliness of our brochures, the institutionalized new-member orientations, the self-serving nature of our membership hustlings." Eventually, though, we will watch as discerning newcomers move on. If we were to ask them why they have left, they might be able to put it into words: It seems to them that the predominance of functional, institutional considerations within the congregation diminishes their chance of finding what they came hoping for.

Perhaps we will mute the word of judgment and the word of call that this situation affords us. Instead of heeding the message, we will drown out an important learning opportunity by saying about newcomers, "They just don't have the same sense of responsibility nowadays that people used to have back in the days when we arrived."

Callahan identifies this search for community as one of four foundational searches basic to all people. In our new times, he says,[4] congregational leaders must creatively wrestle with ways their communities can help people along on their personal pilgrimage through all four of these searches.

The four central leadership tasks Callahan names are each related to one of the foundational searches. These leadership tasks are:

(1) *Helping people in their search for individuality and identity–their need to rediscover and reclaim power in their own lives and destinies.*[5] He presents an analysis of our time's dislocation of power away from individuals and from local settings. Decision making becomes centralized and bureaucratized. People's lives are affected by what has been decided, but they feel they are incapable of influencing the outcome. This sense of powerlessness leads to apathy,

Think of the leaders in your congregation. How are they identified as leaders? Do they have titles? Do they hold identified positions of responsibility? Is their age a factor? Their number of years in the congregation? Their reputations? What personal qualities, different from these things, indicate they are leaders?

What happens in your congregation to help people see themselves and others as unique and valuable individuals? How much of this "just happens" and how much is planned?

a feeling of anonymity, and a submissive inactivity. Callahan sees much of the bickering that goes on among people in workplaces, schools, community organizations, and congregations as coming from displacement of an increasing societal anger about this loss of a sense of power. When that anger is turned inward on the person instead of into the outward world, it shows as depression. Sometimes it manifests itself as an increasing demand for power. That can be healthy and constructive, but it can also be chaotic and deadly.

In Callahan's view, the work of congregations in relation to the search for identity involves helping individuals gain a deepening sense of selfhood, of distinctiveness, of being a unique and worthwhile person on one's own, separate from whatever groups may have one's loyalties. It also involves helping people recover a sense of autonomy and personal power, not of a self-centered and self-indulgent kind but rather a responsible moral centeredness.

(2) *Helping people, in a relational way, to build "communities of reconciliation, wholeness, caring and justice."*[6] Callahan holds that individuality is discovered in community. Community, he says, involves giving and receiving care; it involves sharing with other people, belonging to family and friends. The search for community is also a concern for heritage and roots, for participation in a generational and historical continuity—past, present, and future. "Amid the alienation and loneliness of this time," he says, people come to congregations as part of "a desperate search for community." Congregational leaders are called to transform their congregations into communities where estrangement, anger, and grief are overcome; where fragmentation and dislocation are healed; where people care for others in covenantal ways, with expectations of one another and with mutual forbearance; and where injustices and prejudices are addressed.

Reflect on two or three times you have felt deeply connected with others in your congregation. What was the occasion? How does your experience in the congregation compare with your experience in other settings?

Have there been times in your congregation's history when estrangement and anger have been generated within your congregation? Are there particular areas in which this tends to occur? Which areas?

(3) *Helping people find a sense of meaning in everyday life.*[7] Callahan sees people struggling against a sense of insignificance in their lives. They want to feel that their actions make some difference, that they have a contribution to make, and that they are of value in the scheme of things. People need a theological sense, he says, a feeling that they are being drawn forth as part of God's mysterious unfolding process. The emerging congregation must help people in what he calls this "technological, intergalactic civilization" to resist the pull into conformity with those around them, or, conversely, to resist polarizing against those others by clinging rigidly to one set of issues and answers and claiming universal superiority. The question of meaning that people bring into their congregations is fourfold: What is my mission in the world? What will help me increase my understanding of others and of God's majestic creation? What are my central convictions and my religious community's convictions? And, how does my life participate in the issues of this age and in the life of God?

In what ways do your personal convictions differ from your congregation's traditional or official convictions? What problems are there with such differences?

(4) *Helping people move together "to meet specific concrete human hurts and hopes—both societal and individual."*[8] He calls this the foundational search for hope. In response, it is the leader's task to guide people into a sense of mission. That leadership involves helping people to envision a possible future in which at least some of their ideals and longings find fulfillment. He says that God's kingdom is here in every instance of reconciliation and wholeness, caring and justice. But the kingdom is also not yet fully present.The emerging congregation helps people experience hope, mission, and a sense that their lives, their values, and their actions are taking part in that kingdom's presence and in its advent.

In what ways does your congregation act to meet societal and human hurts and hope within the congregation? Outside the congregation? How are you or have you been involved ? How might you become involved in the future? Is there something holding you back?

For the Life of the Spirit

No matter what words they use, people come to congregations—traditional, mainstream, liberal, evangelical, fundamentalist—seeking to gain energy for the life of the spirit. In Callahan's helpful typology, they come for a sense of individuality, a sense of community, a sense of meaning, and a sense of hope. It is helpful to take this as a standard by which to measure our own congregations.

In far too many situations, when congregational leaders pay attention to the arrival of newcomers and try to assimilate and retain them, they do it in the ways described earlier. Contrast that approach with what Callahan has told us people are seeking and what he says will energize them spiritually.

Paul Tillich said that anything can become "transparent for the divine." I understand this to mean that any thing, any event, any circumstance can, theoretically, be an occasion that opens into deep insight and a profound sense of holy connectedness. It is conceivable, then, that appointment to building and grounds, finance, and membership committees, election to the presbytery, or joining the finance canvass committee could bring people closer to God, giving them a sense of individuality, community, meaning, and hope. In practice, however, people don't often report such an outcome from their involvement with a congregational committee. Instead they often seem sad, disappointed, or tired. They wait out their terms. Some faithfully do the task, but they carry it out as a piece of secular, worldly work done in the church as folks who don't have much interest in the life of the spirit. There are those who don't show up at the meetings and some who never get around to doing the job assigned them. They begin to complain of burnout. A few hold on to the committee positions, some for a sense of power, some because of their unmerciful inner sense of duty.

Many, however, look forward to the day when they will be replaced by an unsuspecting newcomer.

The problem here may well be the congregation-wide assumption that Carl George said was class bound and power driven: that a job will get them in and keep them in. Again, from that passage by Callahan: "Jesus said, 'I must be about my Father's business.' He did not say 'busyness.'"

Not busyness! I will express my perspective directly and bluntly: it is preposterous to assume that most people come to a religious community because they want to be part of running another organization. People don't climb the mountain to the guru's hut because they want to be on a committee or because they can provide sound advice on balancing budgets. The seekers go there, as they come to our congregations all along the theological spectrum, to find help living and deepening their own unique lives in the spirit.

How busy are you? Too busy? Not busy enough? Just about right? Is your congregation frenetic? Inert? Lively?

Did you come to the congregation to get more active in your life? To meet people? For help with your spiritual life? With your family's spiritual life? In what ways have these hopes been fulfilled?

Members as Consumers

For years Quakers have said they are waiting for a grand change to take place in the churches. They await a remarkable transformation. They say they hope for "the abolition of the laity." Something of great importance is being said here, but it is a strange saying. The Quakers don't mean by "abolishing laity" that they want to cast out all the laypeople, leaving only clergy. They mean to end the conventional distinction between clergy and laity—where clergy have the power to do ministry, and laity have no power but to be ministered to. Thus, Quakers want to abolish the conventional role of the laity, with the result that all members of the religious community will know they have a ministry. But not necessarily a *church* ministry; rather, a *life* ministry.

Our growing ability to imagine the end of the customary distinction between clergy and laity harbingers the emergence of a radically transformed church.

Decades of experience working in professional ministry, in both small and large congregations, have gradually convinced me that real depth in congregational life
cannot exist if members view themselves, underneath
it all, as consumers. The Quakers say they await an
end to "armchair Christians," an end to what one congregational consultant has spoken of as "congregational
life as a spectator sport." Members of congregations
as spectators and as consumers? Such a view suggests why the conflict between clergy and laity in many
congregations can be summed up as an argument over
whether "the customer is always right." "Right," perhaps if congregational life is understood a certain way.
"Right," but not really living the faith.

Though mostly unnoticed, the consumer image of
church membership is widespread. When questions
arise, for instance, about how to orient potential new
members to congregational life, the usual response is
to provide a list of services people can expect.

"Here are the committees that serve you."

*What messages are
given to people—
either intentionally
or unintentionally—
that tell them what
they can expect in
their relationship
with the congrega-
tion? What expecta-
tions are they
given?*

"Here are the services the church will perform
for you."

"Here are the people on the staff or in the leadership who will meet your needs and strive to fulfill your
expectations."

And if people leave a congregation because they
are unhappy, the conversation often centers on what
they wanted but didn't get, which needs of theirs or
their families were not satisfied, which services were
not provided well or not provided at all, or how they
were treated insensitively by the "clerks" or "service
personnel."

In this commercial model of church affiliation, the
customer (parishioner) has needs and seeks to have
those needs satisfied by receiving service from a
congregation. The dissatisfied customer complains that
what was provided was not of good quality or was provided rudely. On their side of it, the "service personnel"

(staff and clergy) can be heard privately complaining that this particular customer is the type who simply cannot be satisfied. Just about everybody agrees, however, that underneath it all, congregations and their leaders exist to supply services to meet the needs of consumer members.

Professional Spiritual Care Providers

In this consumer model, the needs of the "customer" are often identified as "spiritual needs." Ordained clergy are generally understood to have been trained professionally to meet the spiritual needs of a congregation's members. Congregation members may disagree about the meaning of the word *spiritual* or about what proportion of the clergyperson's time should appropriately be spent on administrative versus spiritual concerns. But few people will dispute that the clergy are providers of professional services for the members, who are the consumers. If the member-client comes to church to learn, the clergyperson supplies information or insight as teacher. If the member-client needs support or guidance, the minister supplies it as counselor or therapist. Members are consumers. Clergy are professionally trained "spiritual care providers."

This approach presents at least three problems. In a large or growing congregation, the "caseload" can become too big, leading to clergy burnout and to choices and actions that eventually stunt congregational growth. Second, no matter how many ordained clergy or other staff there may be, if staff members are considered the church's care providers, the congregation's ministry will be energized only by the gifts of clergy and staff, not by the wealth of gifts of congregation members. Third, professionalization itself can pose the problem that community development expert John McKnight identifies as "disabling help."[9]

What four or five major gifts come to the congregation from the clergy? From the staff? From the laity? Are some of these more obvious than others? How might this be changed for the better?

In his book *The Active Life,* educator and spiritual guide Parker Palmer speaks about this phenomenon, suggesting that professionalism has sometimes had the effect of lowering people's estimate of their own abilities and has set up and perpetuated an unhealthy dependency—on clergy and others. Professionals speak of themselves in ways that stress competence, high standards, a service ethic, and personal sacrifice. But Palmer raises a very different perspective on professionalism:

> A professional is a person who has invested long hours and much money to develop an allegedly rare ability that others can be convinced to need and to purchase. . . . We professionals get caught in the . . . spinning of those interlocked illusions that too often trap the professional and the society in a vicious circle of nonsense. . . . [10]

Palmer also states that there is something like a conspiracy among professionals to keep themselves in business by "making sure that society never runs out of the problems that guild members know how to solve."[11]

Which professionals are most criticized in the nation at large? In your community? In your congregation? How do you explain this?

One way this is done is by employing a technical or esoteric language when describing the problem and its possible solution. That way, he says, every profession—from ministry to metallurgy to mental health—assures that only it can understand either diagnosis or cure. Relatively common, normal difficulties can be made to seem so serious that nothing ordinary people try could be of any use.

> When society at large is schooled to think of elemental human sadness as "a depressive syndrome," what layperson has the confidence to offer its victims help? Instead, we turn to the very professionals whose opaque language helps keep them in power by making laypeople feel inadequate. . . . [12]

There is a way, then, that professionalization of care can shut people off from the in-built, God-given impulse toward health and wholeness that stirs within the world and within and among people in relationships. Sometimes well-meaning but overly responsible clergy have become identified as the healing's source rather than simply one of its many possible agents. When I was young and early in my ministry, I was told by an older colleague that congregants would not be happy if anyone other than clergy came to visit when they were in the hospital. It was to the detriment of my ministry and the congregation's ministry that for too long I believed what he told me. It meant that the load I carried wore me out and that I always felt guilty because of all the people I missed. It meant, also, that too many patients waited in vain for a visit. My colleague's comment also resulted in a far too narrow understanding throughout the congregation about who had the wherewithal to carry out its ministry. In all probability, it fostered the view that clergy hold in their possession a magic that, in reality, is no person's possession because it is already God-implanted in the world and within and among a host of persons.

Give two or three examples of ways a professional has helped in your life. Share an instance in which personal or professional help has had a harmful effect.

> The grieving person does not need professional technique so much as a restored confidence in the elemental grace of life, the grace found in community or in nature or in the self.[13]

In contrast with this view that an elite have exclusive access to healing power, we witness the popularity and remarkable effectiveness of Alcoholics Anonymous. For decades this lay-led program has carried on its work of helping people through horrendous circumstances and of supporting individuals and families as they learn how to walk a new spiritual path. Its persistence and its success raise questions about the assumption that only professional ministers can be spiritual caregivers.

Make a list of the various self-help groups or activities you can think of that are not led by professionals. Are there more or fewer of these than you supposed? How well do you think they work?

I do not suppose that all clergy will be comfortable with what I am saying or where I am heading. Many laypeople will be unsettled by it as well. Dramatic changes are taking place all around us, and this book, written in hope, is part of the sea change that I believe the church is undergoing.

Nearly 500 years ago it was declared that God's creative and redemptive energy is more generally available than some people in established positions of ecclesiastical power wanted to acknowledge. We find ourselves in a not dissimilar time of disruption for the Christian church. It sometimes seems nowadays that everything is fading off or falling apart. But I am comforted and challenged by the memory of Martin Luther who said that at the very moment when it seems that all is lost, we are on the verge of being saved. ("You exalt us when you humble us. You make us righteous when you make us sinners. You lead us to heaven when you cast us into hell. You grant us the victory when you cause us to be defeated."[14]) I believe there are signs that God is stirring anew in this time and that the means of grace are indeed becoming more generally accessible. The rapidly expanding sense of what ministry is and who can do ministry are sure signs and expressions of this hopeful change.

Who carries out ministry in your congregation? What fraction would you guess is done by those who are paid for doing it?

Kennon Callahan senses and proclaims that hope. He sees the changes of these times in a larger context. "Each new generation," he says, "must carve out an understanding of ministry that matches with its time."[15] Because of that, he opens his book with some startling words, but he doesn't think of them as "striking prophecy." To him and to me they seem but "quiet declaration" and "gentle confirmation": "The day of the professional minister is over."[16]

The Training of Ministers

Over the years, mainline and liberal seminaries have taken as their task the training of professional clergy as spiritual care providers, most of whom were expected to carry out their work in a congregational setting. In some of those schools the meaning of *spiritual care provider* is extended so that the care is not to be provided solely for those within the congregation, but for the larger society, offering prophetic vision and critique for distorted social structures. In recent decades some seminaries and denominations have adapted the curriculum to provide training for community ministers, that is, professional clergy who perform their ministries without a primary congregational focus.

My training, both in seminary and afterwards, was always for parish ministry. The training seemed to fit and to make sense for about the first one or two decades of my more than 30 years as lead minister. But during the most recent decade of my ministry—even as my congregation's membership neared 1,000 adults—I had a growing sense that what I had been trained to do and was doing well was not what we now needed. This is not meant to repudiate what had been accomplished. Many lives were touched and enriched. We had good times in religious community. We stood together and witnessed to an open, responsive, worshipful, expectant way of the spirit—and that made a difference in individuals and families and in the larger community.

But through it all and especially in that last decade, I was unsettled. I was sensing that something else was needed. I participated in workshops and seminars. Gradually I learned a new orientation as I worked within my congregation with laypeople who were organizational development specialists and experiential educators in their professional lives. I read the successive books of congregational consultants Lyle Schaller and Kennon

Callahan as they came along. I followed the publications of Loren Mead and the Alban Institute. Over a number of years I studied with Rabbi Edwin Friedman who helped train me to think "systems" and to get the sense of what leadership is within a systems framework—the kind of thing that Peter Steinke has presented so well in his book *Healthy Congregations: A Systems Approach*.[17] I also resonated with what some of what Bill Easum was writing.

Over and over, throughout the range of my ministry, but especially during that third decade, I noticed myself trying something new, finding new and different ways of interacting with people. These ways of being the pastor were at times unconventional and quite different from what seminary had trained me to be and do in professional ministry. I found myself able, at times, to decline invitations to take charge. Sometimes, even in situations that were quite eager for my tending, I could restrain myself from rushing in. I wasn't shirking my responsibility. I was experimenting to see if I could evoke and energize ministry from others.

Is the pastor in your congregation always available?

It was not easy for me to restrain myself, and I had to deal with distressing pangs of guilt. Functioning in that way still goes against my extroverted, activist temperament. But in one situation after another, when I was able to resist the "rescuer impulse" and bear the discomfort of not responding, other people began to be concerned and to involve themselves in lively, unexpected ways. And sometimes these others were among the last I would have predicted would become involved in such creative ways.

Think of some times at home, in your workplace, or during your volunteer efforts when you held off doing something and others then stepped in and took over. How did you feel about it? How well was the responsibility carried?

Out of these experiences, I developed and led a workshop some years ago as part of a clergy conference exploring the issues involved in congregational growth. I called my workshop "What the Minister Needs to *Stop* Doing to Promote Church Growth." Now I would broaden the topic and call it "Ways Clergy Can Stop Doing Ministry So the Congregation's Ministry Can Thrive."

Here are some illustrations of the things I presented:

Clergy should stop attending all meetings that take place within the congregation. I started out eager in ministry and very interested in what was taking place. It seemed to me that by attending all the meetings I was signaling my sense that whatever was happening in the congregation was important. It was also a way of showing my concern for the people who were making it happen. It took a while–quite a while–before I noticed how my "virtue" of perfect attendance was having a limiting effect on the growth of the congregation. I was inadvertently determining the number of gatherings that could take place in the congregation within one week, or on any given day. The maximum number of gatherings had to be limited to the number that one person–*this* person–could arrange to attend. Certainly there couldn't be more than one event going on at the same time, because the minister can't physically be in more than one place at a time. When I gave up the idea that I should or could be omnipresent, more gatherings began to be scheduled, and the activity level of the congregation became full in ways it couldn't have before. Then it became my challenge to determine which of the meetings really required my attention and my participation. I also learned that *I didn't need to attend meetings from start to finish.* I could be present for a while to listen, to speak if I had something to say, and then to move on.

A final illustration of the importance of "not doing" relates to supervision. A staff member comes to the pastor and describes a problem. The description ends with the customary question from the staff member to the supervisor: "What shall I do about this?"

It took far too long before I began to notice that there was an odd pattern to such conversations.

"We have this problem. What shall I do?"

My response, in the early days, would be to offer a specific recommendation for action: "I think you should do such and such."

If no staff member is present during a meeting in your congregation, how well do things flow? What problems do you see with that? Do staff members see problems with it that you do not see?

"But," the staff person would often reply, "if we do such and such, then this unwanted consequence will occur."

"Oh, right, I can see that," I would say. "Well then, we should do this and that."

"But if we do this and that, this other undesirable result will come about."

Then, at some point and at long last, I began learning to shift the conversation and to respond differently. "We have that problem, you say? What have you decided to do about it?" And then, on my better days at least, I would listen to the response. I would listen and I would push myself past my own ego needs—whenever possible—and, instead, affirm the other person's solution. Restraining myself and then, whenever possible, accepting the other person's solution involved a letting go of control that even today does not come naturally to me or, I'd guess, to very many clergy.

Give an example of a situation in which you have stopped yourself from intervening, and the result was disastrous. Give an example of a time it worked out well.

My inner discipline for situations like that has been to give myself a talking to: "This other person is bright and charged with real responsibilities. She or he may not deal with the situation as I would, but I can't and don't want to be dealing with everything. She must have ownership of her own decision-making 'territory,' but that cannot happen for her if my ownership keeps being asserted as I tell her how to do it 'better.'"

There are times, of course, when the pastor really must intervene. But those are far less frequent than we tell ourselves, and they should be kept to a minimum. People cannot be trained or encouraged to take responsibility if the supervisor continually moves back in to solve the problems people encounter as they work. When the minister continues intruding, the process trains lackeys, and lackeys are incapable of carrying responsibility of their own. It is the supervisor's responsibility to resist accepting another's responsibility, even if the other person invites such taking hold.

"It is a difficult problem, but I expect you will figure it out. If you need a listening ear while you work it through, I'll be here. But my preference and my expectation are that you will tell me how you have handled it, after it has been taken care of."

Such a stance does not abandon leadership, but rather moves leadership to a higher level. It lets go of the decision-making and problem-solving prerogatives and encourages others to take them over. This approach to leadership within a congregation begins the process of sharing the ministry with other staff and with lay members. It advances congregational life by opening new dimensions of ministry and identifying new challenges, such as the need to train others in ministry and to establish appropriate matches between people's gifts and the work that needs to be done.

Loren Mead writes of the emerging need and emphasis in congregations:

In your congregation, with whom do you share your accomplishments and failures in congregational work? Is such sharing a formal expectation? In what ways is it helpful and in what ways is it not?

> Ministry in the past age was the task of the professional in the pulpit. . . . The people generously supported that ministry. The new ministry is the task of the people where they are involved with life–at work, at play, at home–wherever. Clergy who used to BE the ministry, and were trained to be the ministry, do not know how to train the new ministry, are unsure how to support it, and often cannot even get out of its way.
>
> Similarly the people are not universally enthusiastic about the new responsibility that is theirs, are not clear what they are to be and do, and are often afraid to get started.[18]

What problems would you have with accepting the responsibility of ministry? What possibilities or promise does it hold for you? For others?

Evoking the Ministry of the Laity

Strange though it may seem for a clergyman to say, I can find no better arena from which to derive an image of the shifting role of the ordained clergy than from the music life of the church. The professional minister of past generations was like the trained vocal soloist. But suddenly the contemporary need is for a choral sound. Dramatically different skills are needed to evoke a good sound from an ensemble than are required for singing solos.

The great new challenge for seminaries will be to train leaders of *shared and mutual* ministry as distinguished from the customary *solo* ministry. Given the degree of emerging interest in shared ministry, seminaries ought to stop teaching outdated models of ministry. They should take an active part in research and experimentation aimed at helping students develop the theological orientation and the practical skills they will need if they are to be effective leaders in congregations of laity sharing in ministry.

To what extent are pastors trained to evoke ministry? To what extent are they trained to do the ministry?

Among the practical abilities that seminaries should help to develop are skills in gifts discernment, in evoking the ministry of others, and in training, coordinating, and supporting lay ministry. Seminaries need to address the issues and dynamics related to the ministry of the congregation as a whole.

In the past, skilled leaders were thought of as people with loyal *followers*; we now need to think of leaders as those in whose presence *leaders* appear. Similarly, ordained ministers must be trained to be people in whose presence *ministry* appears. Ordained clergy must weave their presence and their absence into a spell that evokes the ministry of the laity.

But it is not only better seminary training that will be required. Congregations will need to reconceptualize themselves in order to reinvent themselves. My experience in leadership with the Minnesota congregation tells me that this is a massive undertaking, requiring skilled initiatives by lay and clergy leaders throughout the entire life and structure of the congregation.

For congregants to move from a perception of themselves as *members* to that of *ministers* will require time and will be helped by occasions for reflection and conversation. The Minnesota congregation proceeded towards this goal by inviting members to a three-session "Finding Your Ministry" workshop, which was designed by a team led by church member and organizational development consultant Linda Giesen and me.

What preparations are being made in your congregation to create new possibilities for the ministry of the laity? If it is already being done, in what ways are ministry opportunities made known?

In this 14-hour experience (two long evening sessions on either side of an all-day Saturday session), people were invited to move, with 10 to 20 others, through a series of powerful exercises and activities designed to help them increase awareness of their *gifts* (their unique combinations of talents and skills), their *values* (what touches them, moves them, calls to them, disturbs them), and their preferred *arenas* of expressing these. In creating the workshop design, we came to the conclusion that a person's gifts, values, and arenas of expressing these constitute the primal source and ground of an individual's life's ministry. We reminded ourselves that people are energized and fulfilled when they interact with their world from within that core of themselves. And further, we realized that they are most likely to live effective lives when they are helped to live from that inner center. Rather than helping new members discover how the congregation can serve their needs, we sought to energize them by encouraging them to learn who they are in their God-given uniqueness, what they can become, and how they may be able and ready to be of creative use in the world.

In addition to what it may have done for the person's association with the congregation, we found that this workshop provided the significant and unusual benefit of offering participants the opportunity for self-reflection and self-discovery—all too rare in a culture that doesn't seem to value these very much.

'By invitation only' we offered people the opportunity to participate in this workshop, and we began by inviting the congregation's most visible and most widely respected leaders. We believed—correctly, as it turned out—that these were the people most likely to bring about widespread and lasting congregational change. They had the personal and reputational capacity to influence opinion among the main body of the congregation. By the time 10 to 15 percent of the congregation had become engaged in the workshop's process, we saw that significant change had taken place. Among the membership, the general perception was growing that the congregation is really a system for evoking and supporting the ministry of the laity.

Misgivings are inevitable as the transformational process takes place. One concern that recurred was worry that we were adding new work to what was already going on. How could we now expect the congregation to undertake the major new job of helping people into a process of discerning their gifts and values? Even those who caught the excitement of moving to support people in expressing their gifts more fully in their lives correctly cautioned that the congregation was trying to do something it just didn't know how to do and wasn't organized to carry out.

What resources do you know about or can you identify in order to learn more about lay ministry in your congregation?

Another objection we heard again and again was from people who liked the idea but said, "I think the congregation is on the right track with this new emphasis, but frankly, I don't have time for ministry. I'm too busy being a mother (or too busy at a job) to take on a ministry too." There were delightful moments too, however, when because of something we said or asked, those same people began to light up with a dawning realization that being a mother or a teacher or being effective in their work is the very kind of gifts-based, worldly ministry that we were saying the congregation should encourage.

If you were pressed to identify your own two or three areas of ministry at present, what would you say?

We must return now to the question raised in the beginning—the question about the lasting value of what congregations currently do with and for people, about the value of busywork by the pigeon-control committee, and even about weighing the value of the deliberations of presbytery, board, or council. We must ask whether maintenance of the ecclesiastical organization is really a spiritual path and, if it is, whether we can assume it is the best path for every newcomer.

Today's congregations have a need for, and I believe are on the brink of, a paradigm shift from *membership* to *ministry*. We will see more and more of this shift as the new millennium unfolds.

In the *membership* paradigm, people become members of an organization that promises to deliver them spiritual care. They are asked to perform institution-maintenance tasks in order to keep them involved.

The *ministry* paradigm, in contrast, engages people in inward gifts discernment and outward expression of their core of gifts and values, alone and with others, in personal and shared ministry—in their homes and congregations, out in their communities, among their friends and among strangers, and in their workplaces.

Letting Go of Numbers as Proof of Success

Looking back, I notice a change that began for me about 15 years into my time as a parish minister. I think I can specify the very weekend it happened. By then I was preaching to Sunday congregations of 250 to 300 people, and the lovely Minnesota sanctuary felt excitingly full for most services. On the weekend the change began, I was in Grand Rapids, Michigan, where I had been invited to be guest preacher in the pulpit of the Fountain Street Church.

It was Sunday morning. I had been dropped off early and I was waiting outside the office of Dr. Duncan Littlefair, that congregation's minister of many years. I was a bit nervous about my upcoming sermon but eager to meet Littlefair, about whom I had heard so much. I knew the congregation had grown tremendously during his decades of leadership there. I knew he preached to a congregation of more than 1,500. I had already been shown the peaceful, uplifting sanctuary. Now, as I waited, I could see through the open door of Littlefair's office. I was surprised. It was a tiny space—tiny indeed for the leader of one of the largest congregations in America.

There was something else truly puzzling. I was amazed to see that man's desk. Again it was tiny when compared to mine. But most unsettling of all, there was only one sheet of paper laying there. It looked like a "while you were out" telephone message.

Soon Dr. Littlefair arrived and we moved into the work of the morning, readying ourselves for the worship service whose leadership we would share together. But I was vaguely disoriented. I had encountered a paradox and it threw me into a search for an explanation. "The leader of one of the largest congregations has one of the tiniest desks." Back home I had a large desk and a large office. You could tell that an "important young minister" sat there. On that desk in my office in Minnesota there were other signs of how involved and concerned I was. There were piles of paper—tall piles, many of them. There was always at least one that was on the verge of toppling. There in Michigan I puzzled over it. "Well, this is strange: that one unsettling piece of paper."

On that day, the paradox of that one piece of paper in that large congregation hit me and began opening me to new understandings of congregational leadership.

I didn't discuss these observations with Dr. Littlefair that day, but he and I *did* talk about money. I remember him saying to me, "Every time clergy get together, the subject of money comes up within the first few minutes." I have observed in many gatherings over the years the accuracy of his statement. Or if not money, then the talk is about busyness—numbers of people in attendance or the number of meetings attended.

It is difficult to avoid doing this. North American culture is attuned to numbers and its habit is to measure success by the heft of the bottom line. Not only do clergy evaluate their congregations that way, but so do many lay leaders as well. I suspect that the frequent clergy conversations about numbers is not simply a wish to boast, but at times expresses the anxiety of the parish minister who is always concerned about showing good results during whatever official or unofficial evaluation is coming next.

The issue of evaluation of congregational life is a very difficult one. So is the use of figures in the weighing of what is going well and what is in need of improvement. I agree with neither those who would do it all by numbers nor with those who say numbers don't tell anything about the quality of life in congregations.

Evaluation criteria should be established consciously and intentionally so that important things are measured and appropriate measures are used. Suppose the goal of a congregational project is that parents and children will interact in a more satisfying way. The success of that project is not demonstrated if we hear that 27 parents attended the training, or that there were 12 more people than were expected. The goal was not 15 or 12 or 27 parents attending. The goal was "more satisfying parent-child interaction." It is possible to measure degree of success in meeting that kind of goal—maybe even in numerical terms. To do that, however, reflection and conversation will be needed in advance to solve the difficult challenge of finding appropriate and adequate means by which to weigh the project's results. How can "more satisfying parent-child interaction as a result of this project" be truly demonstrated? Congregations are easily distracted by impressive (or disappointing) numbers that don't have much to do with the intended ministry goal.

Duncan Littlefair, countering his own tendency to be anxious over financial concerns in the congregation and, incidentally, indicating a proper use of numbers in congregational life, was heard to say, "If we come up with less money this year for church operations than we want, well then, part of this year's unique challenge will be to find ways of doing significant ministry with less." With this attitude, numbers aren't important as an objective indicator or determiner of success. Rather they are a stimulus for heightened commitment to the success of doing significant ministry.

Letting Go of the Sacred/Secular Split

Congregations often sustain a familiar division of labor, reserving the "important" spiritual work for the clergy and leaving the "mundane," institution-maintenance work for the laity. One justification given for this division of labor is that it maintains the secular institution of the church while freeing the clergy from distractions with practicalities and keeping the laity involved and engaged.

The problem with this is reflected in the fact that one person recalls the old saying as "God is in the details" and another recalls it as "The devil is in the details." As we wonder which it is—and realize that it can be either—we come to see that details are a fundamental theological and spiritual concern.

The sharp, often unthinking, distinction between the sacred and the mundane can cause difficulties in congregational life. This is because the institutional aspects of a congregation constitute its "body," and in both Judaism and Christianity the body is seen as sacred, the vessel of God. The mix of body and spirit, sacred and mundane, human and divine—though difficult for some people to encompass—is an inevitable outcome of historicist and incarnational approaches to the spiritual life. There are many ways of misunderstanding and misapplying the idea of the church as "the *body* of Christ," but the image offers a striking way of raising the questions: How much of the church should be off-limits to clergy? How much should be prohibited to the laity?

If the institutional aspects of a congregation are its body, and if the body is the vessel of the spirit, then work in the institutional, organizational aspects of the church's life is surely a form of "ministry," a tending of the "sacred body" during which sustenance and energy are derived. As Maura Williams, a leader in both administration and spiritual development within the Minnesota congregation, wrote:

> . . . it ill-serves our people for us to continue in the habitual conception of weekday congregational activities as mere secular adjuncts to worship....[We say that] work meetings, leadership gatherings, adult education experiences and the like are not best seen as secular adjuncts. These become further opportunities to encourage individual giftedness and to stir the spirit toward greater richness.[1]

Jesus on Letting Go

And I will ask the Father, and he will give you another Advocate, to be with you forever.

This is the Spirit of truth, whom the world cannot receive, because it neither sees him nor knows him. You know him, because he abides with you, and he will be in you.

"I will not leave you orphaned; I am coming to you.

In a little while the world will no longer see me, but you will see me; because I live, you also will live.

On that day you will know that I am in my Father, and you in me, and I in you. (John 14:16-20)

The Poet Emily Dickinson on Letting Go

A death blow is a life blow to some
Who, till they died, did not alive become;
Who, had they lived, had died, but when
They died, vitality begun.

Emily Dickinson

Letting Go While Sounding a Warning

We were paying a quick visit to a young family in the parish. As the seminary intern and I pulled up to the curb to park across the street from their house, we saw that everybody was there: mother, a lively woman who taught children with special needs; father, a quiet man who also taught school, second or third graders I believe; six-year-old Maggie; and three-year-old Mike. We waved, called out greetings as we crossed the street (a busier street than I would like to live on) and we held onto the railing as we climbed the concrete steps to join the parents where they were working. We walked across the grass on a leveled terrace in the steep hill that was their front lawn.

We weren't there long and this event happened many years ago, but on that day I witnessed something that I admired, something that set an example for me which, at times, has called out my better nature.

As we four adults talked, Mom and Dad—but especially Dad—kept an eye on the children. Maggie was a few feet below us down the hill. Mike was a few more feet below her. She was hefting a vinyl ball the size of a small balloon, and it was easy to guess what she was thinking. Throw the ball to Mike. Throw it down the hill to Mike.

The lawn sloped down below Mike to the sidewalk. The sidewalk then followed along the edge of their lawn and spilled another 100 feet downhill before it leveled out.

Little Mike was ready to play. Maggie was ready to throw. We adults were talking. Dad was watching. Her arm went up. Dad spoke. His training and savvy as a teacher shaped the words to perfection—not the controlling or judgmental words, "Maggie, don't do that foolish thing!" Not "You're going to risk hurting Mike, who might run into the street." Not "Be a good big sister." Just this. Just right. Intervene because it's necessary, but step out of her way as you do. Let go of any impulse to undermine the girl. "Maggie," he said, "use your best judgment." Gifted girl that you are—the message was—I'm reminding you that now is a time to use your gift of good judgment.

Maggie paused a second. She then lowered her arm and, affirmed by what her father said and by the good judgment she had just made, she scampered down the hill to hand her brother the ball.

A Personal Prayer for Letting Go

(The reader is invited to spend some time in private reflection, making notes in the four empty spaces below. While the contents of the sheet may be shared with other people if desired, the primary purpose of this exercise is personal meditation and prayer.)

I have learned, creative God, how to make a difference.

Since late in my childhood I have noticed that what I've said and what I've done has affected others and influenced the way things turned out. I am grateful that you have called me into life and that, even to this day, you have given me the chance to be a player in this, your awesome world.

I am proud of some of the effect I've had in recent days and weeks, when a word or an action of mine energized another and made a good difference for them or for a situation's outcome. I'm proud of myself that:

When this was happening...   I said or did this...   And this resulted...

-          •   •

-          •   •

-          •   •

I am pleased when I remember those times. But there are other effects I've had that I am sorry for:

When . . .   I said or did . . .   And this was the result . . .

-          •   •

-          •   •

-          •   •

I pray that, whatever hurt these actions and words of mine may have caused, your wisdom, which is far greater than mine, will transform them into good use, as so often you have done with the unworthy words and deeds of people over the centuries.

And I know, O God, that it isn't only my words and my actions that have had a helpful or hurtful effect. Sometimes my choice to keep silent and my decision not to act have made a difference too.

Sometimes I just stood there and I kept quiet. It caused harm, or at least I missed the chance to make things better.

It would have helped if I had spoken or acted when:

•

•

•

But there were times when I practiced the discipline of letting go. I bit my tongue. I kept myself from reacting, and my silence and nonaction had an important and good effect:

I didn't do anything or say   And the good outcome was...
anything when...

•   •

•   •

•   •

In the beauty and bounty of your world, O God, you have made me one of your wondrous and complex creatures. I laugh at myself at times. Sometimes I'm troubled by the effect I see I have had. But all in all, I feel proud and puzzled and privileged to be as multifaceted, as gifted and complicated as I am.

So again I say thanks for the privilege of being . . . being here . . . being here together with others in this time of promise and challenge. Difficult though it is at times for me, I let myself go into your bountiful wisdom and pray that I may be one with you as you continue, moment after moment, to create this world anew. Amen

CHAPTER 2

From Entitlement to Mission

Entitled to Influence

Robert Frost wrote: "Home is the place where, when you have to go there, they have to take you in."[1] Lacking a clear sense of their reason for being, many congregations have allowed themselves to become places where, although they won't even take a particular person in at home, they have to take that person in at church.

Some people are always willing to accept the open welcome they find in a congregation and turn that welcome into their own personal and perpetual entitlement. They feel entitled to have a say, to stop things from happening, to criticize without accountability, and to prevent changes that might unsettle and upset them. They feel entitled to "do their own thing" whether or not it fits with the congregation's sense of shared mission. They feel entitled to possess and dominate turf of their own—a committee or a task force, for instance.

Some who come to congregations have been hurt by horrendous circumstances. They tell of early experiences of home and of religion that can be adequately understood only as "spiritual abuse," sometimes accompanied by physical abuse. But it is not always as it appears. Some people adopt the stance of victim because they know intuitively that certain organizations—churches among them—grant power to meekness.

In what ways is criticism taken seriously in your congregation? Are critics free to speak? Are others, including staff, free to disagree openly with the criticism? In what way is criticism well used? Poorly used?

An unspoken and unexamined supposition in congregations is that scales of fairness can be returned to proper balance for church members and that past hurts can be canceled by affording people recognition and privilege—perhaps by giving them an important congregational assignment, as if offering power to these folks were a kind of reparation for what someone in some other place, some other congregation, some other time, has done to them. In these congregations leaders are probably not aware of what American poet John Ciardi was calling attention to in his dramatic 1959 poem, "In Place of a Curse."[2]

> At the next vacancy for God, if I am elected,
> I shall forgive last the delicately wounded
> who, having been slugged no harder than anyone
>   else,
> never got up again, neither to fight back,
> nor to finger their jaws in painful admiration.
>
> They who are wholly broken, and they in whom
> mercy is understanding, I shall embrace at once
> and lead to pillows in heaven. But they who are
> the meek by trade, baiting the best of their
>   betters
> with the extortions of a mock-helplessness
>
> I shall take last to love, and never wholly.
> Let them all into Heaven—I abolish Hell—
> but let it be read over them as they enter:
>
> "Beware the calculations of the meek, who
>   gambled nothing,
> gave nothing, and could never receive enough."

What do you like about the Ciardi poem? What do you dislike about it? Does it point to anything that you have seen in your congregation?

It is perhaps unfair to say that those who stay on too long in congregational seats of responsibility contribute nothing. Indeed, often they have given a great deal. In the situation here being discussed, it is generally assumed in the congregation that certain leadership positions belong in perpetuity to particular people and that no one could ever adequately take their places. A fairly certain sign that one is dealing with a congregation of this kind is the frequent joking one hears to the effect that the person would like nothing better than to have somebody take over his or her position of responsibility. But it never happens, and that person's tenure continues on and on.

Is it difficult to end one's term of responsibility in your congregation? What explanation can you give for this? Can you think of an even deeper explanation?

There is an unspoken assumption—perhaps related to this tendency to grant certain individuals unlimited tenure—that congregations should alleviate the feelings of powerlessness that gnaw at people who must cope with vast forces beyond anybody's control. A congregation might think it should do this by providing a bit of turf for as many of its members as possible. People will then sense they are having an effect upon the world and making a difference. A church committee or task force, it is supposed, is such a bit of turf, a place of significance.

Because they are not attentive to the power dynamics of organizations—perhaps especially those of their own church—many congregation leaders are apt to distribute power to members based primarily on "entitlement" considerations. They will then make appointments because of what they think will keep emotions from stirring, what might upset or please potential appointees, and because of what those people might personally want or need. They will give far less consideration to the range of skills or other personal characteristics that will be needed to carry out the task. Instead of noticing that they are helping to perpetuate "organization by entitlement," the leaders view their way of filling volunteer positions as a sign of their church's friendliness, its willingness to be accommodating, and the care with which it avoids hurting people's feelings.

Who determines who will assume the various responsibilities within your congregation? Are the criteria for selection widely known?

This situation is complicated by the fact that in many congregations nobody is in a position to do anything about

*In your congrega-
tion where do you
think most people
would fall among
the following three
opinions? (1) The
pastor tends to be
too controlling. (2)
The pastor should
take a firmer stand
in congregational
operation. (3) The
pastor and lay
leaders usually
strike just the right
balance. What's
your opinion?
Give two or three
reasons for your
opinion.*

volunteer entrenchment or to undo a poor match between a person and a job. Partly this is so in
nonauthoritarian churches because there is general
agreement that the clergy should not interfere. Many
think it would be best for the laity if clergy are held in
check and limited in their power. In some settings, the
pastor is unable to be of any help because the checks
and balances relegate the clergy to organizational in-
effectiveness. As an explanation for their practices,
people (clergy and laity alike) explain that ordained
ministers must be limited in their authority because lay
leaders need sufficient room to be fulfilled in their lives
and to carry out their own ministries. The argument
seems to be that if the clergy have authority, then the
laity will not have any.

People with significant influence in a congregation, but who are swayed by entitlement and conflict-
avoidance considerations, do not usually think of themselves as leading an organization that lacks the courage to call folks to account for their performance or
that is afraid to declare that it is time for new leadership. They do not notice that their decisions and their
avoidance behavior help to determine the congregation's
character. The message proclaimed by that stance is:
"This congregation advocates avoiding the more difficult issues involved in interacting directly and authentically with others in community."

Inadequate Missions

Congregations get into the habit of granting leadership
positions and recruiting volunteers on the basis of entitlement because the congregation has an unclear or
misguided sense of its mission. The unarticulated, unconscious mission of many congregations is found
among the following:

- to provide a friendly place where conflict avoidance is a high priority, where there is tacit agreement not to notice the less-attractive "shadow side" of people's behavior, and where people do not acknowledge openly bothersome characteristics they find in people with whom they frequently interact
- to provide institutional power as reparation for victims of spiritual abuse or those who present themselves as victims
- to provide an organizational outlet for people who need to feel they are making a difference in the world
- to attract ever-increasing numbers of people into membership in the congregation and to retain a large percentage of these by granting them work to do to help sustain the communal and institutional functioning of the church (as discussed in the previous chapter)

Give an example of a conflict situation in your congregation that was dealt with well. Are there conflicts still quietly present, though unresolved? How do you know this?

I believe that none of these are worthy, but congregations are willing to settle for these unspoken pseudo-missions because the question of mission raises issues that are difficult for many congregations to face directly.

The fundamental question is "What shall this congregation do?" The appropriate answer to this question is "Do what God is calling us to do." The problem starts here because there are different understandings of the call and in many congregations in these times there is only a hazy sense—if any sense—about who is authorized to interpret the nuances of the call. What kinds of services shall we provide? What kinds of challenges shall we offer? Who will make those determinations? By what standards will success be measured? Who will do the measuring?

Congregations avoid these and related mission questions for a variety of reasons. Many congregations would rather not face the question of authority, so in order to avoid it, they pass over the mission question. This avoidance, however, is at the base of much of the conflict that later erupts in congregations because of underlying disagreement about who has authority to do what.

Another reason congregational leaders avoid the question of mission may be associated with the recent widespread use that businesses and secular enterprises have made of the language of vision, shared vision, mission, and intended outcomes. It is ironic that some congregational leaders shy away from these concepts, which have long been associated with religion, because it seems to them they would be following a secular trend if they were to use those terms in relation to congregational concerns.

What is your congregation's history in missions work? Does it focus on local or distant arenas? What new arenas might the missional life of the congregation address?

Perhaps, too, there is a lingering association of "mission" with projects carried out on far-off continents. Maybe the word is emotionally associated with the inappropriate missionary zeal of other eras, sometimes hell-bent on imposing an alien way of life or system of belief on native peoples "for their own good." Or perhaps church folks are wary of the language of vision and mission because they fear that, when it comes from them, in contrast with business people, it may seem to be attempting to reflect a wild-eyed, unrealistic, overly idealistic approach to life.

In spite of all this, the time is ripe for congregation leaders, together with their full membership, to consider what they believe their congregation is there for, what it stands for, what it hopes to bring about, and what conditions it wants its presence to help establish in its community and its world.

Vision Evokes Mission

A people's vision is their image of the way the world should be. Their mission is the part they are moved to play in bringing that vision into reality. The overriding vision that drives the Christian church has been expressed in symbols that continue to return over the ages and that century after century are questioned, reinterpreted, freshly understood, and reappropriated. Some key symbols for that vision are: the kingdom of God on earth, the reign of God, God's way, redeemed existence, life in Christ, life in the spirit, spiritually oriented living.

How do you react to these phrases? What feelings or memories do they evoke in you?

The church's large mission—its task, its calling—is to be a way (some would say, *the* way) of lifting up and proclaiming that vision, of being a midwife to its birthing in the flesh here among us.

A particular congregation's mission is to do that very thing locally, to do it by means of a sustaining and challenging religious community, to do it in specific ways that reflect the history and heritage, the tone, the style, the needs, the strengths, the gifts, the values, and the aspirations of those specific people in that particular locale.

Mission Discernment

Congregations that sense their identity as communities of call and that can point to specific ways they are answering that call tend to be healthy and strong. The greater the clarity they achieve about the particular mission they have taken as their own and the more explicit they can be about the specific outcomes they seek, the better it will be for them.

A major responsibility of congregation leaders—laity and clergy—is to keep a keen eye focused on the far-reaching vision. Given the disagreement nowadays in many places, including congregations, about who has authority to make important decisions, wise leaders periodically engage the membership in a well-designed, congregation-wide process of mission discernment. Such a process will ensure that the congregation has had a significant part in determining its local mission. That participation will increase the number of people who have ownership in it.

Samples of the kinds of questions the people will explore in various settings during the mission discernment process are:

- What are we doing by default that we value and could do better were we to commit ourselves to it as part of the mission we actively claim?
- What negative impact are we having on the community that we would end were we to become intentional about our actions?
- What does continuity with our congregation's history suggest that we should be doing?
- What new efforts are calling us that we are not now attending to?
- What needs do we see in our culture or reflected in our community that we are moved to respond to?
- What assets of our congregation (human and other) stand out as a good resource for carrying out our mission?
- What service involvement do these assets themselves suggest?
- What issues and practices related to the spiritual life should we include in our community's way of being?

The overall design of the discernment process will include a final sifting and winnowing by participants and leaders acting together. This will help move the process toward closure, culminating in the eventual achievement of general congregational consensus.

Such a process will take more time than some would like to spend, far more time than in the (perhaps imaginary) earlier days when one authoritative voice could pronounce what the congregation should do and all the members would stand up and march. Though the more participatory and democratic process recommended here has not been typical over the long history of the church, it takes into consideration the new independence of spirit in our time, a spirit that is very promising and, for the enthusiastic visionary leader, at times quite maddening. Choosing to acknowledge that independence by designing participatory, democratic ways for the congregation to do its work is not merely a lofty, idealistic choice. It is, as well, a savvy leadership strategy that has adapted itself to the reality that most people in our day require a sense of ownership before they will energetically participate–even in church.

Have you experienced situations in the congregation or elsewhere in which a person or a few people could declare a vision and the whole group would go along? When was that? Who were the people? How did it turn out? What causes such a situation? Could this happen in your congregation today?

Once a congregation has achieved consensus and commitment about its mission, it is time to move into a new leadership mode by finding congenial and effective ways of keeping things moving forward in line with what the people have decided.

A sample of one congregation's statement of mission comes from the Minnesota congregation I served. It is intentionally concise and sweeping in its scope: "To be a religious community engaging people in a free, experiential and inclusive way of the spirit."

Are people in your congregation empowered to move forward once a decision is made? Are there ways of stopping leadership from carrying forward what has been broadly decided? Share what you know about this.

Those who worked through the process of composing this mission statement know "by feel" how much meaning it contains. They would each probably be able to write whole paragraphs on each of the key words. They know that, singly and together, the words reflect a great deal of the congregation's history and its faith. The statement conveys meaning to people outside that community, as well, but people outside can never receive the richness that its principal authors feel when they read it or speak it from memory.

What do you like about this mission statement? What would you add or remove to improve it?

Any congregation that engages in a mission discernment process will have a similar experience. It is
one sign that such a process binds the people together
in a palpable sense that they are a community of shared
meanings.

Review and Outcomes

It will be helpful now to review the mission discernment process by considering the way a typical congregation might proceed when it has left behind its customary institution maintenance or entitlement identity
and begun the move toward mission. What is described
here is not the way every congregation will move, but
it illustrates a number of important stages that can be
expected.

Early in the process the people are likely to attune
themselves to what is troubling about the state of the
world, their culture, life in their community, their experience within their congregation.

What problems in our time, not named here, would you add as something your congregation and other congregations should try to deal with? How could the congregation be involved? Who else might share this concern?

Perhaps they see human beings, lost in mass movements and markets, being treated impersonally. They
are aware of many influences at work inviting people
into a banal and superficial quality of life experience.
They perceive a widespread resignation, a hopelessness, in young and old alike, about the possibility of
something better. They may also feel the disconnec-
tion of people from one another, from their history, and
from their community.

It is important that during this process the people
of the congregation come to notice the underlying reason why they are troubled by these qualities in the
present world. I believe it is because in their soul as a
people they have been graced with that prior image
we mentioned earlier in this chapter—the image of a
redeemed world, a better way the world could be.

They can be encouraged to open themselves in

empowering ways to the energies that have been released over time by the heroic witness and the accumulated wisdom of the figures of the tradition. These acknowledged and unacknowledged saints of the church (some who have obeyed and some who have rebelled) have struggled, with a degree of success, to live "in the kingdom," to embody part of that vision—life in the spirit, life God's way.

The congregation develops a sense of its own calling in relation to that vision. It senses that it is drawn toward a mission of helping to make a way for the coming of the envisioned world. It works to express in its own words an understanding of the mission it has discerned. In committing itself to being as concrete and rigorous about its mission as is possible, the congregation moves to identify in advance which indicators will be signs to its members that they are being faithful in carrying out their mission. What outcomes, they ask, will show them and others that what they are working for and praying for is indeed stirring in our world?

Two Theologies of Congregational Life

This book does not purport to present what all would agree is the single Christian view of the place of a congregation. I am spelling out the implications for only one of two prevailing understandings of *congregation*.

The view I do not defend directs attention toward a realm beyond this world. It posits such a transcendent world as our spirit's proper focus. It downplays events that take place in this present realm of space and time in our lives and communities. It sees all this as passing and basically insignificant. It has minimal expectations for our lives, seeing our will as sinfully self-centered and our efforts at communal life always tending toward unfaith and brokenness. Congregations exist for worship of the Lord of the other realm. Our intentions and our efforts here aren't of much importance and won't make much difference. The Lord of the other realm is great and majestic and vastly beyond us and beyond anything we can envision or accomplish. Life in the other realm is the true goal of life in this one.

Do you know people who look at things this way? Do you tend to agree or disagree? With whom do you discuss theological issues? Are you able to state your position clearly?

In the view that focuses on another realm, significance is seen to dwell beyond the sphere where the people are. Power and answers are also seen as coming from beyond the people. Such a view provides a perfectly apt, metaphysical support structure for empowering a view of congregational life in which wisdom, power, and authority come from above and beyond the realm of the laity.

I am not challenged or inspired by such a religious outlook. Indeed, along with increasing numbers of others in our time, I find myself disheartened by it–almost disillusioned.

I am stirred and motivated, instead, by another view that is also age-old. It is incarnational, as Christianity has suggested is appropriate. It finds God in the events of life, the holy in the particular and the local. It sees creation continuing in and through events in nature, events in history, and in our communal and personal experience. This view finds God in this-worldly occurrences, as the Hebrews did. It believes that humanity has a part to play in the ongoing process of divine creativity. The new that emerges into the world through our very lives, alone and in concert with others, is part of the creativity of God.

During the 19th century, American poet Walt Whitman expressed something of this outlook when he said he "found letters from God dropped in the street."[3] Ralph Waldo Emerson, the 19th-century transcendentalist philosopher and essayist, gave a feeling for the presence of the sacred in this-worldly occurrences when somewhere in his journals he wrote, "God is clothed in the flowing robes of events." Emerson's remark says more, perhaps, about what to expect from life events than it reveals to us about God.

What comes to mind when you picture such a "robe" for God? How would events feel to you if they were woven into that robe?

If the sense of congregational mission being presented in this book seems too much concerned with transformation of this world or if it seems to emphasize humanity's contribution to the creative task, it is not because I disbelieve that a far grander pervasive creativity stirs in the scheme of things. I do believe in that creative God and I do believe that God's power stirs in this world, in our lives and times. I believe that congregations participate in that creativity and that our own inner stirrings, alone and in community, are part of the grand creativity–that we can be, and indeed are, co-creators with God.

People who are moved more by the other view I have referred to will perhaps be able to spell out a different understanding of a congregation's mission that is consistent with that view. I am not able to do so.

The view I am sketching here is immanentalist, historicist, empiricist, pragmatic, sacramental, and incarnational. Many others are thinking and writing these days in a similar vein.[4] They are saying that God is truly with us–WITH . . . US. Life in a congregation is missional precisely because God stirs with great possibility in the stirrings of individual persons and in the stirrings of congregations. To share in the life and mission of a congregation can be, for many, the best way for them to sense that their lives are lived within the larger life of God.

In the next chapter we will explore a dramatic moment in early American theology when a prominent preacher made a controversial claim. William Ellery Channing argued three decades after the American Revolution that there is something creative of God in every person–something that is alive and active. He was speaking of the soul. Channing said the soul is good and can grow. This view presented a vigorous challenge to religion's then prevailing negative expectations about people. It countered the sense that the individual was depraved, was stuck in depravity and in dire need of rescue from a realm beyond.

This idea of being stuck in negatives, of realms beyond, and of rescue that comes from beyond recurs in American thought—in theology, for certain, but not only in theology.

Assets of the Community

In our time we find a particularly powerful expression of this attitude in the area of community development where two quite different approaches are being contrasted. The first, which is the most common and the most elaborately funded in the United States, focuses on a community's needs, deficiencies, and problems. This needs-based approach presents information and statistics telling of the depravities and the negativities in a community: crime, slums, poverty, truancy, gangs, drug use, lead poisoning, welfare abuse, teen pregnancy, and the like. The strategy behind that approach is to convince public, private, educational, and nonprofit human service systems outside the neighborhood to develop and to offer programs to deal with the neighborhood's deficiencies.

How are people encouraged to think of the more difficult parts of their community as being dangerous, hopeless, and without inner resources? What resources do exist within those parts of the community?

An important challenge to this widely accepted approach has been developing in recent years because of the work of a group of community researchers and organizers based at Northwestern University in Evanston, Illinois. Their organization, which was founded in 1995, is the Asset-Based Community Development Institute, whose codirectors are John P. Kretzmann and John L. McKnight. Their research indicates that the traditional negative approach and the programs and policies based on such an approach tend to create utterly dependent neighborhoods—"environments of service where . . . people come to believe that their well-being depends upon being a client . . . [and that they themselves are] people with special needs that can only be met by outsiders. They become consumers of services, with no incentive to be producers."[5] I am drawing a parallel here, not only with the consumer model of church life wherein the parishioner is seen as a customer with needs who comes to the congregation to have those needs satisfied by receiving services from others. The more important similarity is in the appraisal of what can properly be expected from people.

In the Web site designed to share its findings, the Asset-Based Community Development Institute shares a research tool it has created called "The Capacity Inventory." The Web site introduces it using these words:

Every single person has capacities, abilities and gifts. Living a good life depends on whether those capacities can be used, abilities expressed and gifts given. If they are, the person will be valued, feel powerful and well-connected to the people around them. And the community around the person will be more powerful because of the contribution the person is making.

Each time a person uses his or her capacity, the community is stronger and the person more powerful. That is why strong communities are basically places where the capacities of local residents are identified, valued and used. Weak communities are places that fail, for whatever reason, to mobilize the skills, capacities and talents of their residents or members.[6]

Kretzmann and McKnight point out that "all the historic evidence indicate that significant community development takes place only when local community people are committed to investing themselves and their resources in the effort."[7] Outside resources will still be needed in these devastated neighborhoods, but they are not the primary need. Those resources, they say, "will be much more effectively used if the local community is itself fully mobilized and invested, and if it can define the agendas for which additional resources must be obtained."[8] The strategy of these community development innovators, therefore, is to discourage our society's fascination with the deficiencies of the people in those communities and to focus attention instead on the skills and assets of the people there. They call this focus on capacities an asset-based approach.

A key element of this strengths-oriented perspective is the development of a "community assets map," which shows all the identifiable gifts of all the people, associations, and institutions in the neighborhood.

> Each community boasts a unique combination of assets upon which to build its future. A thorough map of those assets would begin with an inventory of the gifts, skills and capacities of the community's residents. Household by household, building by building, block by block, the capacity mapmakers will discover a vast and often surprising array of individual talents and productive skills, few of which are being mobilized for community-building purposes.[9]

Their affirmation of the "basic 'giftedness' of every individual" is made tangible when community residents move through the neighborhood inventorying the specific gifts of all the individuals, households, and families in the neighborhood and then placing these on the map. Next they add the assets represented by all the informal citizen's associations such as ethnic groupings, sports teams, as well as all the formal institutions—schools, fire stations, hospitals, private businesses. This assets map replaces the conventional list of needs and deficiencies, and it makes a significant contribution to a neighborhood's sense of its strength and resourcefulness. The people feel themselves renewed, seeing new opportunities and stirring unfamiliarly with creativity and hope.

In another paper, Kretzmann expresses the startling effect the mapping can have on people.

> When all these local community assets, the gifts of individuals, the power of citizen's associations and the resources of local institutions, have been rediscovered, "mapped," and mobilized in relation to each other and their potential to solve problems, then a community previously regarded as empty and deficient will appear on the large civic stage as capable and powerful.[10]

Think of the neighborhood surrounding your congregation. Imagine making a quick map of the neighborhood. What would you include? What would you include in a map of the assets within your congregation?

A Community of Gifts

I believe that a congregation is a gathering of people with God-implanted gifts. It is also an environment, a field of energies, that encourages those gifts into full expression in personal and shared ministry. Because congregations need positive models for carrying out this mission, they can learn from many helpful sources. One of these is the assets-based approach to community change and neighborhood development.

A process similar to that developed by Kretzmann and McKnight can be instituted in a congregation whose orientation to people is based on their assets (their gifts) rather than their deficiencies. It might begin with an invitation to people to consider important interactions in their own life experiences: their relationships with family and friends, children and strangers; what has captured their interest in world and local affairs and in fields of study; what kind of work they do and the way they do it; the volunteer responsibilities they have taken on; the causes they worry about, work for, or support financially; what they are interested in reading; and what qualities they strive for when they encounter people and events. Such a process could help and encourage them to see the many ways they have already, probably unconsciously and sporadically, been living out certain of their gifts and values.

Such a congregational process is a personal assessing of strengths. It offers people a new frame of reference for understanding and prizing themselves as bearers of unique, God-implanted possibilities. It encourages them to understand their earlier life engagements anew—to view them as involving occasions of personal ministry based in personal gifts.

Name three of the most important personal assets you bring to the congregation. Think of three other people in the congregation and make a similar list for each of them.

In encouraging people to notice these things as already a part of their lives, the congregation gives people permission to begin to develop a sense of their personal mission—what they are here for and some of what their lives mean. They are being invited to find the rudiments of a personal call and personal ministry that already exist within them.

Orienting people to themselves in this way can be a key element in the congregation's work. It will provide people a significant benefit not widely available in a culture that doesn't value or promote self-reflection and self-discovery. The congregation, in turn, benefits from its learning about itself and its people in this way, becoming aware of itself as truly "a community of gifts."

Over time a congregation that redirects its energy in this way will find itself reexamining and reevaluating much of what it has customarily done. One area that will likely benefit from such a reconsideration is the congregation's newcomer orientation, because somewhere along the line the question arises, "About what should we be orienting people who are new to the congregation?" If the congregation's primary intended outcome is a well-maintained ecclesiastical institution or people who are kept interested by the offer of positions of power, then newcomers should be oriented primarily to the committee structure, the building, the denominational hierarchy, the congregation's financial needs and resources, and the theological outlook of certain historic persons.

If, on the other hand, the congregation's intended outcome deals with the personal and shared ministries of the laity and the ways they live out their gifts and values, then some form of inventorying and mapping of each newcomer's unique personal gifts and values seems essential.

Many congregations will proceed carefully in making such shifts, both in particular activities like orienting newcomers and in a more general transformation of congregational processes. In Minnesota we inched our way "by feel" toward such a shift. Partly this was because we thought we were alone in sensing the need for changes and partly because we feared it would be necessary for us, on our own, to invent a new congregational schema by which to carry it all out. We knew, of course, about certain other religious fellowships already doing parts of it. The Society of Friends, the Mormons and the Jehovah's Witnesses had long functioned with an entirely or almost entirely volunteer, lay ministry. We had learned of some significant lay ministry being carried out in African-American Baptist, in Lutheran, and in Roman Catholic congregations.

Search the Internet or check an encyclopedia to learn something you didn't know about the lay ministry of one or more of the groups named here. How might another congregation's approach to lay ministry be adapted to your congregation?

Many questions began to form in our minds. How, we wondered, did those groups discern gifts for ministry among their membership? How were the skills of the people matched with the needs of the work? Did they write out a description of the job to be done? What kinds of agreements were made with the person taking on the work? Was all this done informally? Did anyone have a well-thought-through process for doing it?

Then, to our relief, we found that someone in our own part of the country had developed a comprehensive way of carrying it out. She had written a thorough manual (then an unpublished manuscript) that was theologically congenial and was intended for ready application by practitioners in congregations.

The person who had done this significant work is Jean Trumbauer of Minneapolis. She allowed us to borrow and begin to apply her material, which has since been published by Augsburg Fortress Publishers as *Sharing the Ministry: A Practical Guide for Transforming Volunteers into Ministers*. Congregations of many denominations throughout the United States have now used this manual. In it Trumbauer has laid out alternate action plans, including step-by-step recommendations that a congregation can choose to undertake to become a center supporting its members' gift-based ministries. "Communities of faith," she says, "can help people discern, affirm, and apply—within the faith community and in the broader community—their unique combination of gifts."[11]

This Roman Catholic, who has worked as shared ministry coordinator in a Lutheran church and trained for ministry in a nondenominational seminary, sees the coordination of the ministry of the laity as important for many reasons. Primary is her belief that

> we are all called to use our gifts to share in God's ongoing creative and redemptive activity on earth and to grow toward wholeness in the process. The mission of the church is to facilitate this process. . . . Sharing the ministry is what it means to be "church."[12]

Trumbauer's manual is a meticulously detailed, theologically grounded guide for restructuring the congregation to carry out its mission of being the energizing center of a gifts-based shared ministry. The manual sets forth a systematic approach that includes helping church members discern their gifts, helping design ministry opportunities inside and outside the congregation, recruiting people by a process of discovery and invitation, interviewing prospective lay ministers, matching people with opportunities, and training, supervising, supporting, and evaluating volunteer ministers.

Trumbauer has continued and expanded her work more recently through a second Augsburg Fortress book, *Created and Called: Discovering Our Gifts for Abundant Living.*[13] Here again she advocates theology lived in practice. Her theology holds that as we discern our own life's gifts, we are discerning God's presence and feeling God's power within us. We notice that our gifts have an urgency about them; they want to flower forth in useful expression in our living. Her theology, then, expresses itself in daily life lived as spiritual practice. It promises that as we identify and more fully live from the values and the gifts imbedded in the unique person we each are, our usefulness becomes "our bliss."

Name three of your personal gifts that you have simply had to express. Are they still flowering? Which one or two other gifts are getting ready to come forth?

Especially in this second book, Trumbauer expands readers' sense of what a "personal gift" is. Certainly our gifts are what we have and what we know, what comes naturally to us, and what we can do well. But she helps open us toward something more: *our gifts of style* (our introversion or extroversion, our caution or adventurousness, our motivation, and our learning styles) and *our gifts of vulnerability* (body and senses, emotions, values, desires, passions, dreams, weaknesses, and wounds). All these qualities and experiences are holy gifts. Trumbauer helps reconceptualize the congregation as a "community of gifts." She gives many techniques and exercises by which we can work with people in small or large groups, in long- or short-term sessions to help people identify their unique combination of gifts.

We call attention to the Trumbauer manuals because she helps us see that the task of reinventing congregation—as a community of gifts and a community of call—is a massive innovation, and those who embark upon that journey are to be seen as pioneers. The work she has done makes us aware that we are not alone in sensing the need for the reinvention, nor will we be the first to walk that territory. We need not rely on our resources alone or wait for our particular denominational organizations to catch the excitement of these prospective changes. We can join in the transformation that is germinating and springing up here and there among gifted laypeople and clergy in scattered congregations that cross all denominational boundaries.

Dancing the Missional Outcomes

Since things are always moving and changing in a congregation, and since the people there interact in the engaged and immersed swirl typical of human events and communities, one of the most important responsibilities of leaders is to find ways of keeping the sense of mission alive in the congregation. A printed report of the findings of the congregation's mission discernment process won't help keep it alive if it is filed away in a cabinet or gathering dust on the pastor's shelf. A framed copy of the congregation's mission statement done up in calligraphy, though helpful, won't inspire congregational change even if it is hanging in the most conspicuous of places.

What unused gifts of yours could be used in your association with your congregation? Which gifts could be better used in your ministry beyond your congregation?

The outcomes must be built into the very process of congregational activities so that month by month, day by day, the way groups function and the way meetings are conducted assure that people will be encouraged in both informal and formal ways to discern and inventory their personal gifts. They must bring the gifts forward—alone and in concert with others—to meet the challenges and embrace the opportunities of personal and shared ministry.

In the planning that takes place before every meeting, leaders should pay close attention to the agenda (however formally or informally it is to be presented). They must ask themselves how each proposed issue can be handled so the overarching congregational outcomes that arose during the congregation's mission discernment process will find some degree of embodiment in the very course of the gathering.

This important consideration of embodying the mission meeting by meeting will be new to many congregations and can easily be dismissed as "too rigid" or can be simply set aside in the press of events. If it is missed, it is unrealistic to expect ever to see significant accomplishment of the intended missional outcomes.

Congregations are in the habit of separating the content of their present meeting from the long-term goals the meeting hopes to achieve. One widespread consequence of this approach is a startling disparity between people's experience in the meeting and the ends the participants espouse. It is as if the meeting involves a group of people whose goal for the future is that there will be more rhythmic dancing. The meeting's process, however, is limited to sitting and reading out loud to one another from a book on the history of dance technique. If the group's goal is better dancing, certainly the committee members ought to stand up, break loose, and begin dancing with one another. To the extent that they experience rhythmic moments in their session, the overall outcome will have been attained—right then and there.

Think of a time in your congregation (or another place) when a meeting "danced." How many other moments like that can you recall? Describe two or three.

If the desired outcome is ministry, some ministry ought to take place in the meeting. If the intended outcome is spiritual deepening, some deepening should happen as the meeting's agenda unfolds. If the reason for meeting is to develop a sense of wider connection in the congregation, significant connections ought to happen among the participants as the meeting proceeds and later between the group's members and others in the congregation beyond the group.

The leaders are responsible to develop methods for use in the congregation's gatherings that are congruent with—a very embodiment of—the intended outcomes. The more creative the leaders, the more engaging and personally enriching the participants will find the meeting. At times, participants report that the significance of the meeting's discussion reverberated through later interactions and other relationships—because, in the way the meeting's business was carried out, the quality of the conversation rivaled the best moments in a great preacher's homily. It reached a place of personal significance and touched the spirit. The old adage applies even to church meetings: "If your goal is to live in the kingdom, begin by living the kingdom in."

When have you lived "in the kingdom" before most others noticed? How did your doing that make a helpful difference in what happened?

An Outcomes Matrix

The trustees of the Minnesota congregation gathered in a retreat several years ago to articulate explicitly their understanding of the congregation's reason for existence. They identified four outcomes they expected to see as a result of members' participation within the congregation's activities.

(1) *People recognize themselves and others as unique, precious, and powerful.* This is the congregation's stand in response to the tendencies in the wider culture to treat people as mere segments of mass forces. In the context of the congregation, a person senses that he or she is unique and precious; each is worthy deep down (is gifted in specific ways), and is called to be joyfully and expressively alive in his or her uniqueness. This outcome was identified as the congregation's emphasis on the INDIVIDUAL.

(2) *People deepen and develop spiritually.* This represents the congregation's continuing witness against the culture's tendency toward banal and superficial experience. It is the stand that all of a person's

experiences and relationships—dark or bright—can be taken in, accepted, and allowed to have their impact on one's becoming. In faith, the experiences of a person's life can be received as part of a continuing stream of goads and opportunities for reflection and growth. This was identified as the effort to go INWARD.

(3) *People live out their gifts and values in action in the world (in ministry).* This is the congregation's response to the widespread sense of hopelessness and resignation in the surrounding society. By participating in the congregation, people can come to view their lives as arenas in which to give expression to their God-implanted gifts and values—alone in personal ministry and with others in shared ministry—for the exhilaration that comes with self-expression and co-creation, and toward the "greater glory." This is reaching OUTWARD.

(4) *People feel connected to their religious community.* This is the congregation's commitment to respond helpfully to the culture's welter of impersonal interactions that frustrate the need to know whether or not one belongs. People are empowered in the congregation to reach beyond experiencing themselves as God's only child. They come to prize other creatures as God's own as well—both those living and the great community of those who have gone before into history. This is feeling oneself to be a part of COMMUNITY.

What is useful about this list of four outcomes? Is it comprehensive enough? What changes would you make?

When the trustees formulated these outcomes, there was no conscious recognition that what they were doing was parallel to what Kennon Callahan had done in his book, *Effective Church Leadership.* Later we noticed the similarities and the differences. Callahan had identified four foundational searches: the searches for individuality, for community, for meaning, and for hope. He said the missional congregation must strive to help people undertake these primary searches. Here the Minnesota trustees were echoing the goal of individuality and community but were calling for an inward spiritual deepening, which now seems closely related to Callahan's lure toward meaning. And they were calling also for outward expression in personal ministry, which seems to require and rest in something like what Callahan identified as hope.

The Minnesota congregation's trustees left their retreat having framed their congregational outcomes in a matrix (fig. 1).

How can your congregation's activities fit within the matrix? What happens in your congregation that doesn't fit on the matrix? What would you do about that?

Soon afterward we began to notice that the diagram itself helped us continue and expand the significance of the stand we had taken. We saw that, in addition to the significance represented by the outcomes at the poles, the quadrants themselves worked powerfully to evoke new understandings (fig. 2). The individual who deepens inwardly was identified as engaging in *personal spirituality*; whereas, clusters of people interacting together to deepen inwardly were seen as participating in a *communal spirituality*. (This communal spirituality, I later noticed, is related to what author Peter Senge described as "team learning" in his concept of the learning organization.[14] It is related to other things as well, such as "adult education" and communal worship.) When the individual finds solitary expression of her gifts and values, she engages in *personal ministry*. But when she is acting in cooperation with others on the basis of their shared gifts and values, she is engaging with them in *shared ministry*.

The leadership had hit upon a schema that diagrammed the transformed and transformational congregation. Everything that took place within the congregation could find a place on this matrix or, if necessary, could be modified to fit it. If we couldn't make the activity fit, we could ask ourselves if, perhaps, the activity wasn't something we should be spending time on because it wasn't congruent with the congregation's stated outcomes.

The idea of saying no to a proposed congregational activity unsettled some in the leadership, but it

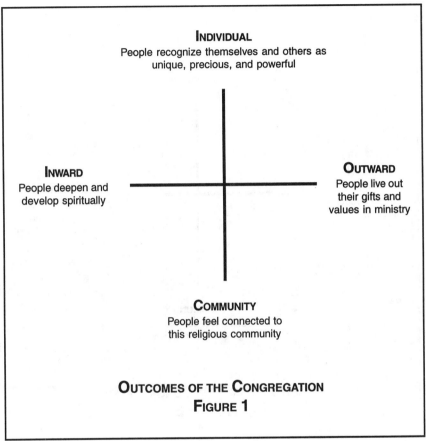

INDIVIDUAL
People recognize themselves and others as
unique, precious, and powerful

INWARD
People deepen and
develop spiritually

OUTWARD
People live out
their gifts and
values in ministry

COMMUNITY
People feel connected to
this religious community

OUTCOMES OF THE CONGREGATION
FIGURE 1

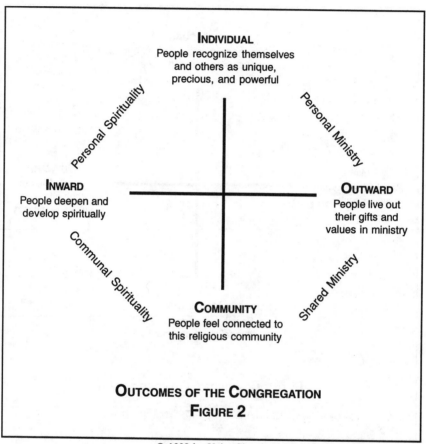

INDIVIDUAL
People recognize themselves
and others as unique,
precious, and powerful

Personal Spirituality

Personal Ministry

INWARD
People deepen and
develop spiritually

OUTWARD
People live out
their gifts and
values in ministry

Communal Spirituality

Shared Ministry

COMMUNITY
People feel connected to
this religious community

OUTCOMES OF THE CONGREGATION
FIGURE 2

wasn't a significant problem because we were now in a position to focus and to say a more energetic yes to activities that fulfilled the congregation's outcomes. There weren't many to which we said no, but there were enough to indicate to us that there was indeed substance to the new statement describing what our congregation intended to be bringing into the world.

Over the course of time, this diagram helped generate new programs, new avenues of communication, changes in the way newcomers were initiated, and new conceptualizations of established programs (as when "children's religious education" broadened in our minds and then in our practice to become the congregation's "ministry with children and youth"). The outcome schema helped the congregation transform itself into a missional religious community. The matrix became for that congregation what the root of its name suggests: matrix . . . *mater* . . . mother . . . womb.

How does your congregation set priorities about what gets done, what gets done very well, and what doesn't get done at all?

As the world moves from the second into the third millennium, we see congregations here and there letting go of their entitlement and institution-maintenance emphases so they can enter upon a gift-based missional ministry. Their resource for that ministry is God given. It comes from the richly gifted lives of the congregation's individual participants who cumulatively form a community of gifts. Expressing their gifts in ministry within and beyond the congregation is an opportunity for their spiritual deepening and participates in God's redemption of the world.

Letting Go of Solo Pastoring

When a senior colleague told me early in my ministry that only clergy were suited to provide the kind of ministry parishioners need when hospitalized, I believed him. There were, however, too many people in that growing congregation for one person to handle all the visiting to hospitals and nursing homes, and I didn't do that work as well as I believed it should have been done. In accepting what my colleague said, I was ignoring a great potential that existed unseen all around me.

I first noticed that potential in a conversation with Mary Anderson. Long a member of the congregation, she had been trained as an RN and was at a time in her life when she had time to take on something new. She is one of those people found in some congregations, someone who seems to know everyone and is known and is highly regarded by just about everyone in turn. She and her family had a generous way of living and entertaining. It was so much a part of their way of being that it was clear it expressed important values and also served important needs of their own. Mary agreed to do some of the visiting. Although her personal gifts and her nursing training would enable her to connect attentively during the visits, we both knew that there were special issues in this kind of visiting that she needed to address. Once we felt that need and started looking for the resource we needed, it appeared. That kind of thing seemed to happen again and again as that congregation underwent its changes. Some called these openings "serendipity." They were workings of grace, manifestations of "a good not our own" that we couldn't see until something shifted in our capacity to look.

The resource appeared in the form of a parish visitor training program sponsored by a community foundation based in our city. Mary completed the training and continued to meet monthly thereafter with leaders of similar programs in parishes of other denominational affiliations.

In contrast to what my colleague had warned, most people were pleased to receive a visit from their congregation's new Parish Visitor, who came also on behalf of the congregation and its minister. Mary reported to me about each visit in brief written weekly reports. She alerted me to emergencies and to situations in which my presence was requested or seemed necessary. I took such calls to me from Mary as a priority and reversed my customary view; I now considered her suggestions that I make a visit to be an "assignment" from her to me.

Some years into the program it became apparent to me that the number of people Mary was responsible for seeing was too many. It was also true that the importance of what Mary was doing for the congregation was being more widely recognized and appreciated. Other congregants were indicating their interest in sharing in the work of parish visiting. Though it wasn't an entirely easy adjustment, Mary agreed to work with me to recruit several other lay members of the congregation as candidates for the training. That done, they were given training, again through the same community foundation's program that had trained Mary. As part of a Sunday worship service, the several trainees who had signed on pledged themselves in this important congregational work and were commissioned as Parish Visitors of the congregation.

Of course, many new issues arose, including the need for Mary to develop her skills as a supervisor of a cadre of workers. Through monthly conversations that she led among the visitors, Mary monitored the quality of care these various individuals were able to provide and she was available to help them work through any difficulties they might be having. The challenges to her grew as the number of workers increased, but so did the richness and variety of care the congregation had become able to provide.

Over the years the program has been through significant changes. We modified the way we train the recruits. Mary herself needed to leave her position for family reasons, and a new skilled leader had to be found and trained as leader. The program—an entirely volunteer, shared ministry that reaches throughout the congregation—continues on. The clergy person could never have been as significant a pastoral presence as the Parish Visitor program has been. Everybody who has a hospital stay and everyone in a nursing home has a visitor. Experience has shown vividly that my senior colleague was wrong and much that is valuable would have been lost to the congregation had I continued to heed his words. With the cadre of Parish Visitors, the congregation was beginning to sense itself as a *community of gifts*, with a ministry truly shared by clergy and laity.

⌒

Letting Go of Being the Instructor

Our underlying faith affects our practice. That is always true and it is true of everybody. Our faith is our inner road map of the world. We interpret what happens, we understand where we really are, and we figure out where we want to go—all according to that faith map. Perhaps our faith has not been thought through; maybe it doesn't fit in all respects with the official faith we inherited from our families; or perhaps it often goes unexpressed. But we can be sure it is there. The more conscious a person is about it, the better.

Sometimes the road map is badly distorted and leads to destructive attitudes and behaviors in personal and societal settings. It may indicate, for instance, "When you get to this place, you should sit and sulk; when you find yourself over here, look for someone to hurt and to blame; if this happens to you, give up and find someplace to hide."

Leaders of faith communities have always known it is possible for faith to change—and it's a good thing that it can. Some of us are called into ministry in order to help people as they enter a process of deepening and strengthening their faith.

It usually doesn't lead to any good or lasting result, however, if we try to impose on others our own self-declared "more adequate" faith we have fashioned or discovered for ourselves. It usually doesn't work, even if our intentions are the best and if what we offer is exactly what the other person really needs. People can change and faith can grow, but the growth won't go well if it isn't connected to and rooted in the other's personal experience.

Unless we are committed to try to maintain the other's faith on his or her behalf, it is wise for us to listen to what the other says, watch how the other acts, and find the parts and pieces of that person's underlying faith that we can respond to.

Paying attention that way will require from some clergy a different kind of ministry. It requires a letting go: letting go of our view of ourselves as the instructor, the expert, the one "in the know," the authority, the good one, the better one, the best one. That's a great deal to let go of, and many leaders, many teachers, and many clergy will find it impossible. Some won't be able to see the wisdom, humaneness, or the strategic value of it.

I don't want them to misunderstand. I am not saying it doesn't matter what faith people have. Nor am I claiming that everybody is equally expert or equally correct. And I am not saying we shouldn't try to influence the faith orientation of others. I believe we can and that some of us are called to do just that.

I say the uniqueness of the other person must first be honored. We do not and should not have command over others in their faith. We move into dangerous and forbidden territory when we attempt it. There is something inviolable about another person. We can ask them what they see, what they think, what they believe. We can share our perceptions, thoughts, and faith with them, as well. It is in such sharing, and not in any kind of dictating, that the transforming God is most likely to be at work.

Rabbi Edwin Friedman said that he, like his mentor Murray Bowen, a family systems therapist, had noticed changes over the years in his view of the ideal therapy session. He was coming to think that during a session the therapist should assert nothing; he or she should only ask questions. That makes more and more sense to me in ministry too, although there certainly seem to be times when people benefit from another's opinion or advice. I confess that the way of questioning doesn't come easy to me. But I notice that when people are given another's answers, they seem either to actively resist those answers or to become passive in accepting them.

In addition, if I give my answer to another as *the* answer, it brings closure to his or her process of seeking, as well as fosters a perception of me as the one who is wise and helpful. To the extent that I really am wise and helpful as a clergyman, I will develop skill at evoking the other's inner wisdom so it can flow from within that person out into the situation at hand.

This skills-building assignment to myself is based in the conviction that the creative spirit of God is present within all people. My well-crafted questions offer an invitation to them to honor their own experiences. The questions create an opening so their own wisdom can surface within them. They then get to be the wise ones.

In ways that giving answers might not, asking questions suggests that mystery is our constant companion. Part of the church's calling is to give people a sense of that mystery. Another part is to remind people that they and everybody else hold insights that humanity needs as it works here and now mapping the outer edge of mystery.

A Chinese Philosopher Speaks of Letting Go in Leadership

> ... of a good leader, who talks little,
> When his work is done, his aim fulfilled,
> They will all say, "We did this ourselves."

Laotzu, ca. 600 B.C.
(from *The Way of Life According to Lao Tzu*, translated by Witter Bynner)

Letting Go of Ministry as an Entitlement

*(This is a sample of the kind of write-up that can be used for ministry reflec-
tion in a small, intentional spiritual community within a congregation. The
incident is imaginary, but the issue it raises is critical for a transforming
congregation.)*

Brief Background

Quite a number of congregations have expressed interest these days in a
shared ministry model of congregational life. It appears to be rich enough an
idea that different people are drawn to it for different reasons. The participants in an informal exchange, which was much longer than is recorded
here, are Alice, Bob, and Chris, who are lay leaders (each from a different
congregation), and Don and Ella, who are clergy. Don is pastor of Chris's
congregation. The setting for this conversation is an after-hours discussion
during a conference all were attending.

The Situation

Don: I'm wary of all this emphasis on the ministry of the laity. I'm concerned
that we are turning authority over to people who aren't always going to follow
through. I can't count how many times I've received a lame excuse from
volunteers who've dropped the ball on something they had said they would
do: "Something important came up" or "I got a chance to go skiing for three
extra days, so I can't finish my part in the project." A few times when I've
pushed them on it, you know what they said.

Ella: Probably something like, "I'm just a layperson, after all. You get paid
for this; I don't. You're acting like one of those moralists; getting kind of
judgmental, don't you think!"

Don: You've got it! I've heard all of those, every one.

Chris: We've been learning that if a "letter of call" is given to the person,
together with a written description of the job, it really helps. That way people
know what's expected and what they are agreeing to do—and when leaders
take the time to do all that preparation, people are more likely to take it
seriously.

Alice: Sure seems like a lot of background work to get a couple advisors volunteering to work with a half dozen junior highers.

Bob: No, not "volunteering to work with . . ." We are talking about being clear with those called into ministry with our youth. It's among the most important things the congregation does. It's worth that extra time.

Alice: I agree. It is important.

Don: What about the supervision and evaluation parts of it? Do you think people will balk at that? They used to do pretty much whatever they wanted when working with the kids. Won't they feel restricted?

Chris: Don't you think that depends on the skill of the person doing the overseeing? I could see it as a way of letting people know their work is really valued—and demonstrating that there are standards for what we do in our congregation with our kids.

Alice: It seems like an awful lot of work on top of everything else church leaders do.

Bob: But what's more important? I think *this* is.

Overall Thoughts and Feelings

The conversation hit upon some crucial issues. It felt good to have it all stated out loud. There were other related issues not touched upon, such as what happens if the overseers tell those leading the junior high ministry they're missing the boat in some respects? By what authority do they do this? Will the overseers be supported or will the congregation's leaders get drawn into it, taking up the advisors' cause?

Reflection Focus

How do I speak about "shared ministry" so people don't think I'm advocating ministry as just another congregational entitlement for the laity but will know I mean "living your faith" responsibly and accountably?

Suggestions for the Reader's Reflection and Discussion

- *After you have read through the full text of the above conversation, go back and read it again, placing a question mark by anything that you wonder about. Put a star by anything that elicits a feeling in you.*
- *Jot down some notes identifying each question or feeling and what in your experience might give rise to that question or feeling. Spend some time thinking about your responses.*
- *Write (or discuss with others) your reactions to the following:*
  - *What themes am I noticing in my responses?*
  - *What do my responses tell me about myself?*
  - *What do these responses tell me about what is going on in my personal ministry?*
  - *What experiences, images, stories, or teachings from my spiritual roots come to mind in relation to this conversation and my reflection on it?*

Letting Go of Being the Wise One

I wanted to see her. She was one of the oldest people in the congregation and had been involved for nine decades, following her parents' decades of involvement. I knew I was about to violate her rule; it had been posted out into the congregation like a "Do Not Resuscitate" order. A gracious woman of the old school, she felt it improper to receive visitors in such an unkempt state. I could imagine what she was thinking. *Days in the hospital have ruined my hair. And these tubes, this rumpled nightgown. No, please—no visitors when I'm in the hospital and out of sorts.*

I had decided I would visit anyway. She saw me as soon as I poked my head into the doorway. "Come in. Come in, Mr. Phillips. Sit down," she said in a familiar lively and gracious way, and always a bit more formal than others in the congregation. "How are your children? Are things going along well at the church?" There she was—at it again. Of course she didn't say it, but I knew what she was thinking. *Mustn't dwell on oneself, especially not one's ailments, even if this hospitalization has lasted three days and the doctors haven't yet explained the trouble with this heart, this old heart. I wonder how his children are . . . what's happening at the church.*

Was she fending me off? Was she crowding in first with her questions to keep me from turning the conversation to her, to her health? And if so, was this really less from graciousness and more from fear? *If we don't talk about cardiac irregularity and physicians' uncertainty, then anxiety can nap out of sight and won't pester me.*

It didn't seem to be so. It felt like more of her natural graciousness. *If he wants to talk about my health, he'll ask me. I'll give him an option: his children . . . How are things. . . ?*

But later, when I asked directly about her health, she answered, "Strange little pains . . . occasional racing beats . . . sometimes hard to catch my breath."

I had known her for a long time. I knew she'd had one breast removed many years before, the other a couple decades ago. I knew she had been having problems with her eye muscles. Now an abnormality with her heart had been added to her other physical problems. I also knew that from birth she had been a daughter of privilege. She'd had many advantages: the best school, travel, no financial worry.

"I've had many wonderful things happen in my life. I've had opportunities most people don't have. Now I've got this health problem. It's another experience of the other side of things. Better that I've had these experiences. They've helped keep me present to the way it really is to be human."

She said all this. Then I asked more questions about her heart and it became clear that if she didn't have the diagnosis, it was because the doctors really didn't know. It wasn't for lack of asking all the questions she could think of. She told me some interesting things she had learned about how hearts work. She was fascinated by the intricate wonder of nerve impulses and blood flow, even about some of the systems that could break down. I could hear a tinge of disappointment in there about her condition, but she was willing and able to be present to the reality of what was happening.

Was I, the clergyman, now supposed to say something wise? She was wise enough.

Was I charged with dispensing some pastoral assurance? It seemed to me that a deep acceptance was already in her.

I had pushed past her official barrier to be with her and that said most of what I wanted to say, except that she was wonderful and her spirit was astonishing, even more so now that I had seen her curiosity in the midst of uncertainty. I said she is wonderful. I said it straight out. I think then we went back once more to technicalities about heartbeats. And then she said the astonishing thing.

"I think if one is going to deteriorate, Mr. Phillips, one might just as well be interested in the process."

Nobody had ever said that. I'd never read it. Never in my experience. The faith beneath it astonished me. She was in the present, here and now. She had been a young girl, a bride, a mother. Now she had become an old woman who was ailing and was still living in a fascinating world, working at being appreciatively aware of it, able to set aside the fearful implications of the information she was getting. ". . . one might just as well be interested."

"Yes, sounds right," I said as, smiling and shaking my head, I walked toward the door. Again, one of the privileges of my work. I had been to visit one of the old wise ones, had come close again to the source, and had seen the wondrous way faith can weave itself into a life—with almost none of the expected words showing to tell you it is there. Just the power and the wisdom, integrated. "What a piece of work!"

CHAPTER 3

From Education to Spiritual Development

Something was wrong in the congregation. The important moment came when a few of us noticed it enough to admit to one another that we were dissatisfied. We were unhappy—in a vague, unclear way—with what our congregation was offering as adult education. Some of us were active as leaders in that very program, so it didn't become a matter of "us against them" as it often does when people in congregations grow dissatisfied.

Several of us—volunteer and staff, clergy and laity—decided we would do something constructive with our dissatisfaction. We would call together a group of bright, committed members and go together on a visioning retreat. One of the congregation members, Linda Giesen, a leader in the adult education program and a gifted organizational change worker, was then employed by the city. She was pleased to volunteer her gifts in designing a process and leading the retreat.

In creating her design, she attentively interviewed those who cared most about the existing program. She needed information they could give her but, by interacting with them in this way as she developed her retreat design, she was also sending a message about the kind of leadership she intended to provide. She was indicating to them that she did not presume to come in as an expert bringing a new curriculum plan that she would impose on the program. She listened.

How do people frame things in your congregation as "us against them"? Give an example. How do you explain this way of handling differences? What would be a better way within your congregation? How would this change be brought about?

She learned. And in that process she gained the trust of those who were most involved, those who might feel the loss most intensely if recommendations for change did later emerge.

During the retreat, which took two weekends set a few weeks apart, she invited people to tell first what they valued most about the existing program. People spoke favorably of numerous interesting classes and good speakers. The support groups seemed helpful to the people who participated in them. The study groups, book discussions, and workshops were often enriching and usually well attended. The part-time staff was kept very busy—indeed was overworked—trying to manage the range of concerns associated with the variety of offerings and the many registrants. All in all, this sounded like a congregational adult education program that would be viewed as successful by usual standards.

Linda then moved us deeper, asking us to recall some of the offerings in which we had participated and to share with the others memories of moments during those programs that seemed particularly significant to us personally. As we went around the room one by one, we heard people speak of times in which they had been touched and moved, moments when even an abstract informational part of a presentation suddenly lit up and caught on fire as a personal insight flashed within the person. The accumulating mass of such reported moments was overwhelming. These people had experiences that had changed them, strengthened them, or led them out of a dilemma and into some new challenge or into a new way of perceiving a difficult problem.

What educational resources are offered within your congregation? Does there seem to be a thought-through set of offerings? How does this work for you? For others? How might things be changed for the better?

The people portrayed a program packed with a broad variety of good things, useful, informative, personally meaningful offerings. In some ways that variety was welcome and desirable. It took into consideration the diverse needs and learning styles of the participants, and the total program had a colorful, wide-ranging feel.

The uneasiness persisted, however, until finally the moment came when the group was ready to speak whatever negatives it had come to share. We took the time we needed. In summary, everybody agreed that the dissatisfaction was this: our adult education program felt catch-as-catch-can, hodgepodge. Nobody could state its mission. Events were often scheduled primarily because someone learned a particular presenter was available. The offerings were all over the place. The program had no center.

"Where do we go from here?" Linda asked. To work toward an answer, she fashioned several small clusters from the group as a whole. She gave people crayons, markers, and large sheets of paper. "Go off and work alone first," she said. "Work on drawing your individual picture of what the overall program will look like in two years. Then work together in each cluster to create a composite picture, and we'll see what happens."

Some people like that kind of activity and do it easily, having fun with it. Others don't enjoy it at all. Pictures were produced, but more importantly, during that exercise a collective sense emerged about what shape we wanted that program to have in the future. *Tell of a time when you were energized by a retreat away with others. What happened as a result to you personally? To others? Did some significant improvements result?* The energy released by those people on the retreat unsettled things profoundly over time and set the congregation on a path creative and innovative beyond anybody's expectation. As it turned out, the retreat helped initiate the massive project we came to think of as "reinventing the congregation," for the participants carried the spirit of that retreat with them and, without anyone initially intending it, the vision found its way into almost every aspect of the congregation's life.

The energy that emerged from that retreat had as its immediate effect the elimination of the congregation's program of adult education. We stopped using those words—as well as the words adult *religious* education. Instead of thinking that our congregation offered many programs, one of which was an educational program, we were putting ourselves through a reorientation exercise of sorts. "If we don't do education," we asked, "then what do we do in its place?"

"We are making of our congregation, instead," we answered, "a center, a resource center, a center for spiritual development." We stopped thinking of our congregation as educating people. We said it exists instead to help people deepen and develop spiritually. Over time we were able to get clearer about what we meant by that.

While I believe it can be said there is an educational dimension to spiritual development, there are at least three widely held, unfortunate understandings of *education* that are detrimental to lively and healthy religion.

First, it hurts religion to associate with the kind of education that functions primarily as a way of adding to a person's accumulating stock of information and concepts. Religion gets to be a matter of ideas about religion rather than the *living* of religion. For example, we may think and talk about the effectiveness of prayer, but never pray. Religion is then rightly dismissed as abstract and a "head trip."

A second sense of education—that of someone full pouring from his or her bounty into someone empty—is also harmful when it is associated with religion. We hear this in various settings. A common occasion for it in the church is when family members or friends make speeches at funerals and memorial services. "Harry taught us always to be cheerful and always to listen carefully to what others tell us." In the sense used there, education is "telling" or "instructing." Harry is credited with a pedagogy that understands him to be the authority who knows, while the rest of us don't know. The implication is that if Harry educates us to be a certain way, we will just go right out and do it. "Harry taught us always to be kind." Education in this sense is more suitable for the religion associated with the Lord of the other realm. Harry is "up" above us, pouring information to us down here, rather than trying to help us become more of what we have it within us to be.

A third understanding of education is that it is the inculcation of community norms. It is socialization. It is being shown the ropes. The learner is twisted and shaped from outside to fit the expectations of others. Religion aligned with this kind of education is diminished to a governmental or a cultural functionary (for instance, teaching people mere manners or teaching mere patriotism).

Each of these—the last two more than the first—is reminiscent of the stance of the theology of the other realm in which significance is seen to dwell beyond the sphere where the people are, and in which power and answers are also viewed as coming from beyond the people. Each of these understandings of education also reflects the same power relation observed by Kretzmann and McKnight in the needs-oriented neighborhood where people are seen as empty, in contrast with the asset-based outlook that sees the people as having gifts waiting to be drawn forth.

How is education in your congregation associated with factual information? How often does an education program involve someone telling others something? How often do groups use the experiences of the participants as a resource for the group's enrichment?

A sense of *education* that is compatible with the notion of a congregation as a center for spiritual development is founded on the classic root sense of the word. To educate (from the Latin *educare*) is to draw forth—draw forth the potential of the person, not bestowing something from beyond, but locating what is already in there and helping to bring it forth.

In our time, we concluded, education is so heavily associated with the first three understandings that we decided to drop the word from our program. It also appeared to us that everything contained in *educare* is better expressed as "spiritual development."

Early American Origins of Spiritual Development

Whatever our religious orientation, our tradition, or our denomination, we in the United Stated need to admit that we practice neither a universal Christianity nor a European Christianity. However much we may have thought about our personal religion, our sense of religion and spirituality derives, far more than we know, from our standpoint within the history and culture of the United States. The events, recollections, and interpretations that constitute this national history have profoundly influenced our thought and our practice. So strongly has the Christian church in the United States been affected by the history and the cultural outlook on this continent, that a relatively high percentage of the population identifies itself as churched or religious or Christian.

It is remarkable then, in the face of the decline of involvement in European churches, to realize how much attention American church leaders continue to give to European theologians. It is remarkable also to notice the other side of this fact: how little many of them know of their own country's almost 400 years of lively reflection on spiritual issues.

An impetus for the original European emigration to this continent was religious: to get away from a limiting European spirituality. Nevertheless, for a long time thereafter–a century and a half at least–the settlers on the eastern seaboard continued to assume that the source and authority for their existence as a people were derived from a place afar, that their power and identity came to them from another realm. They tended to see themselves as rough-hewn colonists eking out a simple existence in a place many weeks' journey by ship from the cities and universities of Europe. Faraway Europe was seen as the source from which culture radiated.

Gradually, American deference to the distant source lessened. That diminishment was expressed politically in the break with the English king and parliament in the Declaration of Independence and the Revolutionary War. Then, a few decades after the new young nation was established, its sense of identity deepened and its own inner resources began to assert themselves. In 1837 young Ralph Waldo Emerson stated it directly when he addressed the Phi Beta Kappa society in Cambridge, Massachusetts, on the subject "The American Scholar." He called for a new and distinct American voice. "We have listened too long," he said, "to the courtly muses of Europe."[1]

A year before, with the publication of his first book, *Nature*, he had made a similar point. The book's opening pages called for a new personal and cultural confidence.

> Why should not we have a poetry and philosophy of insight and not of tradition, and a religion by revelation to us, and not the history of theirs? . . . The sun shines today also. There is more wool and flax in the fields. There are new lands, new men, new thoughts. Let us demand our own works and law and worship.[2]

What changes in your congregation's worship life would increase the power of that worship to help people develop spiritually?

Statements like these of Emerson's still arouse a flood of anxiousness in some people. They hear his words as those of a self-centered or self-sufficient individualist. His recent biographer, Robert Dale Richardson Jr.,[3] disagrees.

> Emersonian individualism is a protest against social conformity, but not against society. . . . [It] is not a blueprint for selfishness, self-aggrandizement . . . nor is it a coded manifesto for the subjection of other persons or viewpoints.[4]

Emerson regretted how readily people settle for the social safety they suppose will come to them if

What do you do that you would consider to be "listening within for the urgings of God"? Share some of what that experience is like for you.

they can discern what others want them to be and to do. He warned that great losses result when that other-directed path is chosen. His call for self-reliance was a call to higher expectations and to a more courageous stand than dependency on others. He urged people to look within themselves, not outside to other people. Listen within, he said, to hear the inner urgings of God.

Emerson was not alone, of course, in linking spirituality to personal experience. Before he attended divinity school, he had read a number of books discussing theology and spirituality. One book, important enough to him that he continued to recommend it to others for many years, was *Life of God in the Soul of Man*, written in 1677 by an English Puritan, Henry Scougal. Richardson excerpts a passage linking religion and inner experience.

> Religion, said Scougal, was not a matter of sect, external duties, or even, "rapturous heats and ecstatic devotions." Religion was, he insisted, a "union of the soul with God, a real participation of the divine nature, the very image of God drawn upon the soul, or, in the Apostle's phrase, *it is Christ formed within us*."[5]

This book appeared on a reading list that was given to young Emerson when he went to visit a pivotal figure in American religion, the Boston preacher William Ellery Channing.

Channing was born in Rhode Island in April 1780, four years after the new nation was born. He studied at Harvard and entered the ministry in Boston in 1803. By 1824, when 21-year-old Emerson was meeting weekly with Channing, the older man had gained a national reputation as preacher, innovative thinker, and controversial leader among New England's liberal-leaning ministers.

Though he has been identified as "the Father of American Unitarians," his greatest significance is not as a denominational leader (indeed, he disapproved of the formation of a separate Unitarian "sect"). He was fundamentally a national spiritual innovator, a reformer, and an inspirer of reformers.

Emerson scholar David Robinson of Oregon State University suggests that Channing's importance is missed if the source of his influence on his times is thought to be a particular set of theological doctrines. "More evocative to his followers than any doctrine he ever preached" was, rather, his repeated insistence on "an imaginative construct that is as much symbol or image as logical affirmation."[6]

So powerful and persuasive was the image Channing put forth that many people in the United States in our day will not understand how fundamental a theological and spiritual reorientation it inspired. American religion did not hold that image in any significant way before Channing proclaimed it. Today it is the attitude the vast majority of us share—and share so profoundly, so automatically, that we scarcely give it a thought. In his 1980 Harvard University address commemorating the bicentennial of Channing's birth, David Robinson lifted up this core image, identifying it as Channing's

> . . . repeated insistence that the soul could grow—that it was a living thing not unlike a plant or animal, and that, like a plant, with careful culture it could be nurtured to develop a certain potentiality of its nature.[7]

Do you think the soul can grow? Tell about a time you witnessed that—in somebody else and in yourself. If you don't think the soul can grow, what in your experience tells you this?

The image Channing offered, then, pictures the soul as a seed. Religion, he said, cannot be reduced to a matter of creed or doctrine. Religion is an activity. It is a process of bringing the "infinite potential" that is in this seed, the soul, "into ever-increasing reality in the moral and spiritual life."[8] He spoke of this potential that he saw in every person as the "divine seed" within. "In ourselves," he said, "are the elements of the Divinity."[9]

Again, this image is common in our day among counselors, pastors, spiritual directors, and many others, both laity and clergy. They carry it into their interactions with people as a largely unconscious working assumption. The soul can grow. Religion is the cultivation of the spirit. It is possible to affect one's own or another person's spiritual development.

If this underlying attitude is common today, it is only after it was worked out in the early 1800s as an alternative to Puritan Calvinism in lively, often bitter, theological battles. Puritan Calvinism by then had gone through many changes from the theology that John Calvin had shaped in Europe some 300 years before. In Channing's day, Puritan Calvinism's "gospel"–its "good news"–unimaginable to many of us in our time, was twofold. First, the person is corrupt at the core ("naturally depraved" was their way of saying it). Second, people are powerless to do anything about it because it has been foreordained and predestined which of us are among the elect who will be lifted out of the condition and which are not.

Have you had any experience with an equivalent of a "Puritan Calvinism" kind of religion? Have you known people who looked at the world that way?

Ideologies and attitudes affect one another. Channing believed that Puritan Calvinism either grew out of or fostered a dour and gloomy sense of life; but whichever way the influence ran, he believed the outlook stunted personal initiative and responsible action. If the soul is stuck and powerless to recover, it is utterly dependent on energies coming from another realm for change to take place. All one's actions in the course of life are at most "preparationist" efforts to ready oneself to be lifted up if those energies perchance arrive from beyond. Within the sphere of the Puritan Calvinist outlook, the two options were either such preparationism or a hope for conversion in a sudden flood of feeling or moment of insight that would bring instantaneous and complete regeneration.

When asked once if he had ever experienced conversion, Channing replied, "I should say not. . . . "

If this had been his entire answer, his stand might have been easily dismissed. But he elaborated: ". . . not unless the whole of my life may be called, as it truly has been, a *process* of conversion."[10]

Robinson suggests[11] that the work of Channing and those associated with him be seen as framing and popularizing a doctrine of conversion that was radically different from that of Puritan Calvinism. In this emerging understanding, conversion is no longer seen as one dramatic experience transforming everything, but rather as a continuing process of spiritual formation and cultivation. This dramatic shift to conceiving conversion as a process has "enormous consequences for the way people approach the religious life."[12]

Tell of a conversion experience you have witnessed, your own or another's—the kind Channing meant or the more instantaneous kind. What is your view of conversion?

We begin, perhaps, to see some of the implications of Channing's gentle image of the "divine seed" and to notice what a doubly radical innovation it was. The human soul is, first, *of God*–not depraved. It is, second, *a seed*–not powerless or stuck. The human spirit has sacred potential within it and that potential can be developed and expressed. The soul can grow.

Life itself was being seen as a dynamic process, a continuing occasion for spiritual growth or development, or in the favorite term of the people in Channing's circle, for *self-culture*.

By *self* they did not mean the psychological entity we think of today when we hear that word. They meant *soul* or *spirit*. And when Channing and his followers used the word *culture*, they were thinking not of art or music or literature, but of horticulture and agriculture–*cultivation*. Self-culture was the cultivation of the spirit–*spiritual development*, as we say it today. For Channing and for many whom he influenced, especially Emerson and others among the transcendentalists, the principal goal of religion was self-culture, spiritual formation, spiritual development.

The image of the church as providing a cultivated field for the sacred seed is astonishing to some people, even today. They find it hard to believe that the church isn't charged with stamping out blight. It is difficult for them to accept that the seed is of God and is good, that it doesn't need external direction or motivation, that the seed is potent, with its own already implanted urge to unfold, to grow, to flower, and to bear fruit.

Channing was agreeing with his opponents in one respect. One cannot earn—indeed, one should not waste energy attempting to earn—one's acceptance or one's rightful place in life or one's place with God, because that status has been simply given with life as grace. But he certainly did not agree with the preparationist understanding: that we work in order to prepare ourselves to receive grace if it comes. This preparationist view went so counter to his outlook that we can imagine him crying out, "Blasphemy! Grace has already come. It was granted as life began. It is the sacred, God-implanted potential within each person. Blasphemy to say 'if grace comes'. . . ."

Early Influence of the Idea of Spiritual Development

Many of those who came under Channing's influence took spiritual growth, usually expressed as "self-culture," as their aim. Books, pamphlets, and sermons of the period dealt with various applications of the idea. Social reform movements were spawned with the outward flowering of the inner divine seed as their core image.

What changes in society have taken place because of a change in religious outlook?

Henry Ware, Jr. was one of the clergy who immersed himself in the idea. He published a devotional manual based on self-culture as its core idea. Titled *On the Formation of Christian Character*, it was widely read as a source of practical advice on living a Christian life as a way of developing in character and spirit.

Ralph Waldo Emerson brought the idea into his sermons, lectures, and philosophical writings. It has been said that American transcendentalism, of which he was a central figure, sought to develop a sense of spirituality in everyday life. David Robinson refers to Emerson as an "Apostle of Self-Culture" because Emerson so widely and so thoroughly affirmed the potential in persons and saw the significance of their lives as coming from cultivating and living out their gifts.

Elizabeth Peabody was a friend and intellectual companion of Channing. She was a teacher who led significant educational reform. She helped shape the educational views of her brother-in-law, Horace Mann, founder of "normal schools" and champion of universal education. She would go anywhere to promote the new approach to early education known as kindergarten, an innovative approach in which the setting or the environment that the school provided sought to draw out the child's potential and expressiveness. (The classroom was seen as a *kindergarten*–a garden not *for* children, but a garden *of* children, one in which children were planted like seeds to grow from within, a field where each child's potential could be cultivated to flower and bear fruit.) Peabody worked with educational experimenter Bronson Alcott, who was the father of Louisa May Alcott. They taught together using techniques influenced by the organic image of the divine seed.

Once again, it is difficult for people in our time to realize how different the world of those times was from ours in some significant areas. At that time the kindergarten was a controversial innovation coming into a society in which many still held to the view of children that had been earlier expressed in an English marriage manual.

The young child which lieth in the cradle is both wayward and full of affections: and though his body be but small, yet he hath a reat [wrong-doing] heart, and is altogether inclined to evil.... If this sparkle be suffered to increase, it will rage over and burn down the whole house.[13]

Peabody and Alcott were innovative educators who based their teaching not on trying to break the wills of such dangerous creatures, but rather in the strengths and capacities they assumed and found in young people. They developed alternatives to teaching "to the tune of the hickory stick." With both children and adults they used conversation as a prime peda-gogical tool by "drawing truth from the facts of com-mon experience,"[14] that is, stimulating the students to speak and express themselves, sharing their own ex-periences and perspectives and hearing those of others.

Margaret Fuller was a member of the Transcen-dentalist Club who shared Channing's view about the importance of ongoing development of implanted po-tential. She was especially interested in helping this to happen among women, and accomplished this largely by holding conversations with women. In that time women were not generally seen as having precious qualities worthy of development or expression. Some of the women involved in Fuller's conversations had never heard themselves express their own thoughts on important matters. In her memoirs she wrote about the importance of lifelong development.

> Very early on I knew that the only object in life was to grow. I was often false to this knowledge, in idolatries of particular objects, or impatient longings for happiness, but I have never lost sight of it, have always been controlled by it, and this first gift of love has never been superseded by a later love.[15]

All these people rejected the idea that people were stuck and unworthy and in utter need of rescue from beyond. They also rejected an approach that put its hope in instantaneous conversion experiences that others claimed would swiftly regenerate a person's entire being. They affirmed the divine presence in people in the form of unique potentials. There were others, like Dorothea Dix, who said she had learned from Channing that no one should be overlooked, that all had potential. She found a divine seed in the indigent insane chained in basements or in prisons, and she did significant work in mental health reform. There was also Samuel May, Louisa May Alcott's maternal uncle, a liberal clergyman who saw a sacred potential being mistreated and wasted in the bondage of slavery, and who joined forces with the then bitterly criticized abolitionists. All these people affirmed that strengths, gifts, and assets were present in all people, and that these gifts were sacred and of God and should be drawn forth in a continuing cultivation and lifelong formation of the spirit.

What problems in our world today—and in your local community—might diminish if the idea of the divine seed were applied more widely?

Spiritual Development in Congregations Today

What would happen if a congregation were to eliminate its education program and to take upon itself the responsibility of becoming an environment in which the holy potential of people is supported and nurtured? What qualities would we find in such an environment? What would it need in order to be a fertile and cultivated field in which the uniqueness, preciousness, and power of the divine seeds people bring can flower? How might it best make the rich ground of culture, tradition, and community available to the individual as a place into which to send roots? What is needed as nurturance in the soil? What is the appropriate balance between cultivation and letting the growth and flowering take its own course? What would constitute

In what specific ways does your congregation provide a wholesome environment for the divine seeds that arrive there? How much of this environment is purposely planned?

pruning? What about the difficult question of weeds? What would grafting be?

Outcomes

Educator and author Michael Quinn Patton,[16] who consults with municipalities, social service agencies, and educational institutions and advocates outcomes-based planning and evaluation, has encouraged such enterprises to ask: "What do you hope to have come into the world in the lives of your students or your clients as a result of your work?" His premise, simple but seldom applied, is that organizations that are clear about what they hope for, will design better programs and processes to bring it about. They will specify at the beginning the end results, the outcomes by which to judge how well they did their work: "We designed our remedial program to help bring most of the students to an eighth-grade reading level, but we find that only a few of them have come that far. In the course of our program most of them have improved to a sixth-grade reading level." Such useful information could take the program developers in any of several different directions as they design revisions in the program for the new group of students coming in the second year.

Having heard about Patton's work, I began to wonder about possible connections with mine. I asked him, as a member of the Minnesota congregation, if he would spend some time with me discussing spiritual development. He was glad to reflect with me on my question. I asked if he thought his notion of outcomes could be applied to a process of spiritual development. Could we go beyond the usual vagueness that surrounds the notions of *spirit, spiritual, spiritual formation,* and *spiritual development*? Could we be clearer and more specific about our meaning? And then, could we ask ourselves an unsettling question? "Does what we do as a congregation really make an identifiable difference in people's spiritual lives?"

Patton thought about my question. He said he believed an "outcomes approach" could indeed apply and would provide focus and an exciting enrichment within a congregation. But he qualified that answer. He said that the hoped-for outcome must be determined by each individual participant for herself or himself. He said each person must be intimately involved in designing the plan and in choosing the experiences and disciplines necessary for reaching the desired goal. He said also that each person, herself or himself, must be the primary evaluator of how much progress has been made.

If you were to set a spiritual formation goal for yourself to develop or to strengthen some personal trait, what would that hoped-for trait be and how would things be better?

This seemed the opening of new doors. I had kept almost out of my awareness my disappointment that every congregation I knew, however lively or healthy, was usually too busy with institution maintenance to carry on anything like a rich, integrated program for the spiritual formation of laypeople. Sometimes I had almost resigned myself to hearing people in congregations speak of their 12-step groups or yoga or Tai Chi or Eastern meditation classes or Catholic-church-sponsored retreats as the source of their support for spiritual development—*but almost never their own congregation.*

But I had been heartened that those in our own planning retreat had noticed that our congregation's program of adult education was uncentered, catch-as-catch-can, and that they wanted to change that. Now here the idea was emerging that the local church could be a kind of in-town, day-by-day retreat site, a layperson's monastery for focusing on formation. A church can become a place set apart where laypeople go to find support and challenge in their personal process of spiritual development.

After my initial conversation with Patton, I performed some quick research, looking for lists of spiritual development outcomes in the great religious traditions. I found some in Buddhist and Christian texts. I carried my Bible to the coffee shop for my second visit with Patton. We agreed that this passage from the Letter to the Galatians could be a beginning of a person's or group's potential long list of possible spiritual development outcomes, a list useful to people as they try to articulate their own personal goals: ". . . the fruit of the Spirit is love, joy, peace, patience, kindness, generosity, faithfulness, gentleness, and self-control." (Gal. 5:22–23)

Choose two traits from the Galatians list that seem to fit for you. Is there another trait that you would like to develop? Tell about all three.

Of course someone might wish to develop other qualities of spirit during, say, the next 12 to 18 months (*im*patience, for instance–the ability to say, "Enough is enough; I won't stand for that from you anymore"). No doubt we could continue adding to such a list of qualities. Someone names forgiveness and someone else says trust, as participants think through a personal plan for spiritual formation and strive for the fruit of the spirit.

I earlier suggested that, in this new understanding, a congregation's orientation session might properly introduce newcomers to themselves, their gifts, and their values. Perhaps without even noticing, they have been carrying on moments of ministry in the way they live their lives. So too, newcomers and others could be provided with the opportunity to focus on what has taken place already in their own process of spiritual development: "What are the large themes of your life's growth so far? What new shapes, what new tones have emerged over time? What do you see as needing your focus in the days ahead?"

Processes can be designed to help groups of people together derive individual "baseline" readings of where each is on his or her spiritual journey at this moment. Each can be encouraged to identify some specific desired quality or qualities of spirit. Congregations can provide structures–classes, retreats, mentoring groups–that offer support and challenge and help people identify the resources they need in order to attain the outcomes they declare for themselves.

Once they have made their declarations, the congregation's program supporting spiritual formation can provide focused, specific encouragement and support, beyond generalized well-wishing: "You say that you want to experience more of the spiritual quality of joy in your life by a year from now. How would you know whether you did? What would you see and feel? What would others notice about you? How can you begin to do those things that will make the development of joy more likely? Or stop doing those things that make it less likely? How can we help? What can we provide for you between now and the next time we gather?" A congregation could offer such structured support and challenge in small groups designed for this purpose.

When you made a significant personal change in outlook or in your circumstances, was there some one person or some group of people there to help? If so, who helped you, and what kind of help did they give?

Most congregations would need to undergo major changes in order to offer such support. Many will not be interested or will not be able to go through the restructuring that would be necessary. This possibility is presented here in the hope, then, that some will be ready to brave the full range of changes required. If that is not possible, perhaps the vision of helping people with spiritual formation will encourage some congregation leaders to initiate less sweeping, but still important, changes.

As the Minnesota congregation moved into its new self-understanding, its board of trustees dispensed with both the finance committee and the office of the treasurer. Before that, they had disbanded their building and grounds and ministerial advisory committees. In some cases staff took over these functions; in other cases responsible individuals volunteered to get the work done or a ministry team was formed whose members used working on those tasks as a way of identifying and addressing issues of their own spiritual formation.

If your congregation had to stop doing two things in order to be of greater help to people, what two things do you think could be done as effectively in a less time-consuming and energy-consuming way?

Who Will Lead?

Some congregation leaders who have found themselves intrigued with possibilities in this book will, no doubt, be concerned about finding people with the skills to carry out the ministries in the transformed congregation.

Some years ago the answer to this concern came out of the blue to me in a casual conversation. I was to be a guest preacher one Sunday in a congregation that had already chosen, but was awaiting the arrival of, a newly called minister. At a Saturday night dinner with two couples who were longtime leaders in that church, all four shared with me that, as soon as the new minister arrived, they would leave the congregation.

Shocked by this news, I asked, "Whatever for?"

"Because we've done it all," one of them said. "Each of us—board, canvass, ministerial search—again and again. We plan to go somewhere else where things will feel new."

Suddenly I saw something I hadn't seen before. I now understood why some seasoned members of my own congregation had faded over the years, had moved on that way.

"You shouldn't go," I boldly said. "Your congregation needs you. But it needs to restructure itself to keep you interested and challenged."

Are you ready to move into graduate-level involvement in some area of your congregation? What area is that? Is there a need within your congregation? Is there room in that area for you?

One of the four people there that evening was a university professor, and her presence evoked the image I was looking for.

"What's needed here for you," I said, "is graduate-level church."

I didn't know then what that would mean, but now I do. In a reinvented congregation such seasoned people will be moved out of the institution-maintenance responsibilities and will be trained as leaders of training sessions, workshops and mentoring groups organized to support individual spiritual development and personal and shared ministries.

We can be sure that some among every congregation's present leaders are already harboring feelings like those of the two couples I met in that other congregation. They are bored with the assignments they have been given and, aware of it our not, they are waiting for someone to articulate a compelling vision of a more significant ministry. We might be surprised at how many people like that there are in our congregation and how many others will come when they hear the call to more difficult tasks that will challenge them to use a wider range of their gifts.

Set free of the primacy of the institution-maintenance paradigm of congregational life and the obligations it generates, the congregation's leadership can undertake the challenging, rewarding, and absolutely necessary shared ministry of mentoring others. They can design and lead spiritual development offerings for others in the congregation. What "curricula" are there for this? Are there materials in the great spiritual traditions? Are there biographies that might help those who desire a specified spiritual development outcome? What kind of training will be needed by those who become mentors? A large segment of the laity could begin asking and incorporating these questions into workshops, seminars, and courses to be offered in the congregation, a congregation now conceived as a center for spiritual development.

Tell about an important mentor in your life. Tell about a person to whom you have been a mentor.

Such courses and workshops should inform and enrich the outward-reaching, personal and shared ministry activities as well. What about activism, the social gospel, worker priests, or the bodily works of mercy of a Mother Teresa? What have the traditions said about the relationship between quietism and action in the world, or about the importance of both private prayer and the corporeal and spiritual works of mercy? Such questions and such resources could be and should be offered by congregations to support people as they design and carry out their plans for personal and shared ministry.

Exploring Scripture toward Spiritual Growth

Some years ago I invited Carl Scovel, then minister of King's Chapel in Boston, to come to Minnesota to preach and to lead a group in a Saturday workshop of his choosing. He chose to lead a Bible study experience, using his adaptation of the powerful method designed by Walter Wink,[17] one that I have since found opens both the biblical text and the souls of the students every time it is put into play. The response of those who attended Carl's session was favorable, and before he left town I told him I wanted to learn the method and begin offering such sessions to the congregation.

He said, "Okay, but if you do it, don't make the mistake I made. Don't be the only leader."

I took that to heart, and with the help of materials another colleague had developed to help laypeople apply the Walter Wink method, I invited several people to attend an evening session and then asked them to learn the method and teach it. Several did.

That was almost a decade ago and the group continues to meet twice a month. During my ministry there, I led no more than two or three classes for that group each year. Lay participants led the other sessions. The leaders are trained and are accountable. The method is solid, and the leaders are not free to set that method aside. They follow it meticulously since it is wide-ranging enough to allow for and call forth the creativity of the leader.

The method is conversational throughout, with the leader asking questions more than providing answers. After people have checked in and shared a ritual opening with candlelighting and centering meditation, they engage with the passage together by reading the text aloud to one another from several translations. After thus hearing the passage repeated several times, people share what shades of meaning, additions, or omissions they noticed in the various versions. A discussion of the text follows, in which the leader asks specific questions. First, with newsprint pad on an easel and marker in hand, the leader asks for negative reactions to the text. People tell what bothered them or what they disliked as they heard the text. As each speaks, the leader writes a short summary of each comment. This can take some time and the leader encourages this important sharing to continue until it is complete. The sheet with the negative comments is torn off and placed somewhere nearby. The same process takes place again, this time with people giving their positive responses and the leader writing down summaries of each. When the group has completed this process, the second sheet is removed.

Name a Bible story that in some special way is about your life experience. Tell what it is about the story that fits for you.

This initial sharing of personal reactions–negative and positive in that order–is a crucial beginning stage in the process. It allows for and is open to the various perspectives that participants (and translators) bring to the text. People notice, at least peripherally, that some of their personal responses are shared by others and some are not, and this tends to keep them from absolutizing about the text and their perception of it. It is sometimes especially touching to sit with a group in which all are free and encouraged to respond personally and honestly, without anyone "correcting" the various feeling-responses shared by the individual participants.

Now the leader asks a series of questions, some about details of the text as it is worded and some to encourage participants to probe further for the meanings behind the words–both the meaning the ancients would have heard and the meaning the group members hear today. The leader mostly asks questions, scrupulously avoiding the role of the "expert," and does not lecture but shares interesting related information gathered while doing personal research and reflection in preparation for the lesson.

The next phase of the lesson is mandatory, though some people are not at ease in leading it. This is a physical activity or a group interaction or both. It can be a dramatization of a part of the text or a debate among the participants. For instance, one team might take a Roman emperor's point of view as opposed to the other team, which might represent the stance of a Jewish peasant. Another physical activity could be having each person use crayons to portray an aspect of the text and then share and discuss the drawing within a small group.

Once at this stage of a session that I was leading on the baptism of Jesus as told in Luke 3:5-22 and 4:1-2, I handed out pipe cleaners and invited people to make stick figures of some aspect of their lives or of some-one known to them—some one or some part they felt needed transformation or revitalization. It was moving to watch as, one by one and without giving any explanation, they silently accepted the invitation I had given. They carried the figure to a large crystal bowl of water, which I had placed on a central table. Each stick figure was tenderly placed in the water and immersed in what looked to be an earnest hope that the person or aspect represented by the figure would find renewal through this symbolic baptism.

For the final phase of the lesson, participants are invited into personal exploration and asked to take time to reflect and write about ways the themes in the text resonate with some aspect of their lives today. The leader decides whether or not to invite people to share any insights or learnings that come to them during this reflection period.

Whether I have been leader or participant, this process has always initiated some personal insight, often of special significance in relation to something I have been dealing with. In ways I never experienced before, the method enables the text to come alive and to speak to me in important ways. Through the process, the Holy Spirit speaks.

In its beginning almost 10 years ago, a group of the initial leaders made the Wink method their own when they put together a set of guidelines in their own words. These are still read as part of each session's opening.

- The goal of these Scripture explorations is to invite participation toward spiritual growth.
- We gather to study the biblical text, which can mean different things to different individuals.
- The text remains the common ground from which various interpretations can emerge.
- Each participant's insights about the text are of value.
- The group illumines the text by comparing and contrasting insights, not by arguing or debating.
- All are invited to participate, but the option to "pass" is respected.
- All personal sharings are to be treated with confidentiality.
- In this "community commentary" approach:
  - there are no wrong answers
  - there are no wrong questions
  - there are many right answers.

What is your reaction, in view of your own Bible training, to this method that relies on community commentary? How is it similar to what you have experienced? How is it different?

"The Basics"

The congregation's overall intended outcomes had been articulated. The matrix was developed and elaborated as presented in chapter 2. It provided a graphic representation of the life of the congregation and became a tool we used with increasing frequency because we continued finding new ways it helped us. One way was to give focus to congregational programs and to open up exciting ways in ministry that hadn't occurred to us before.

We had already designed two workshops, each with a detailed curriculum and each being offered several times during the year by teams of lay leaders whose training, scheduling, and shared evaluation were coordinated by a staff member. The first of those existing workshops, "Finding Your Ministry," has been described in chapter 1. It introduced people to the idea of the ministry of the laity and invited them to consider ways their gifts and values had earlier called them into action or relationship, and to watch for ways a new call might be sounding now. The other workshop, designed by an ordained colleague, Charles Buckman-Ellis, and a group of laypeople, helped families—mostly newcomers—begin to "find themselves" in the congregation as gifted people among other gifted people and to learn about ways the congregation might help nurture them in their spiritual growth and in their ministry.

When we considered these workshops in relation to the matrix, we realized that the two core experiences we had already created matched two matrix poles: OUTWARD and INDIVIDUAL. We were pleased to notice this congruence, but soon we felt the need to do something similar for the other two general areas.

With the guidance of Linda Giesen, we developed the "Exploring Your Spirituality" workshop, offered in three two-hour sessions. In it people are assisted in discovering that, often unawares, they carry with them a number of personal metaphors for their own spirit. They are taught how to work with these unique personal metaphors in relation to the metaphors that derive from the "great code" of the cultural religious stories. They are helped to develop a mature sense of the meaning and significance of rituals and how rituals can both help and hinder a person to live religiously. Participants are encouraged to map the terrain of their spiritual lives, looking for peaks and valleys. They relate what they find on the map to open-ended issues in their lives, issues that they would be willing to address. In connection with this, each is asked to identify a quality of spirit he or she would like to develop or deepen in relation to the identified issue.

With these three workshops being offered by lay ministry teams, we set about completing what we came to refer to as "The Basics." Again with Linda Giesen's guidance, we developed the fourth of these, a workshop dealing with community connection, the heritage of the tradition, and personal religious identity. We called this fourth workshop "Our Way of the Spirit" (fig. 3).

This workshop identifies eight key themes emphasized throughout our community's history.[18] Participants choose one of these as the focus of their exploration and sharing throughout the workshop sessions. They explain what it is about this particular theme that draws them, how it fits with their outlook, and how it may relate to stirrings at this time in their life. They read assigned writings excerpted from traditional sources and look for ways that their theme occurs there; similarly, they look into contemporary sources. They report on all this in a presentation each makes to the group.

As predicted, it was relatively easy to recruit and train people within the "graduate-level church" to be leaders for these "Basics" workshops. The recruits understood that they were being invited to become a new kind of "mentoring elder" in the congregation, a lay guide who would share the responsibilities with other laypeople and with the staff and clergy in carrying out the congregation's ministry.

The training for all these lay ministries includes training in methods for reflective conversation with their co-teachers, including discussion of personally helpful ways of evaluating the outcomes of a workshop session as part of the ongoing responsibility of leadership.

If you were to name the "basics" as they are presented in your congregation, what would you say they are? What do you think they ought to be?

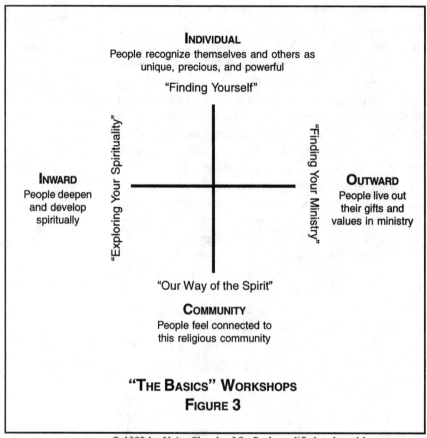

INDIVIDUAL
People recognize themselves and others as
unique, precious, and powerful

"Finding Yourself"

"Exploring Your Spirituality"

INWARD
People deepen
and develop
spiritually

"Finding Your Ministry"

OUTWARD
People live out
their gifts and
values in ministry

"Our Way of the Spirit"

COMMUNITY
People feel connected to
this religious community

"THE BASICS" WORKSHOPS
FIGURE 3

Looking Ahead and Finding Ways to Share

A new life is possible for congregations under this new paradigm. It envisions the congregation as a seminary for the ministry of the laity and as a retreat center or monastery for the encouragement of continuing lay spiritual formation.

In many ways this vision is new, and there are no comprehensive manuals showing how to do it. In this new day of failing denominational bureaucracies, the national organizations are not likely to be of much help. But in the leadership of scattered congregations and among colleagues and laypeople of various religious orientations, there is interest, determination, and skills that we can share.

How does denominationalism help in your religious life? What tangible or intangible resources does your denomination provide?

In Minnesota we did not experience much resistance to these changes, though they were fundamental shifts in what we were doing. We gradually moved our congregation from a source of interesting but rather random educational experiences to an integrated cluster of offerings by highly regarded lay mentors trained to do the work. Perhaps it was the high quality of the material developed that minimized congregational resistance to the change, or maybe it was because we underwent a long, slow process of finding our way and bringing many people into the process.

We can expect significant resistance in many places seeking to reinvent congregations. People will say some of these things: "There are limited resources." "We don't have the skills." "It seems unnatural to have a congregation intentionally focus its energies on ministry and spiritual development."

The odds are that most congregations, in the end, *won't* choose to make the changes. Pigeon control committees and busywork boards are far easier for people to understand, to lead, and even to control. For all these reasons the old committee structure will probably persist in most places.

My hope, then, is that those who are interested in this reformation will continue to help move it along and that those who are technically competent will find long-distance ways–perhaps using the Internet, E-mail, and occasional gatherings–to share their discoveries and to support one another in their work, their failures and their success. To enter into dialogue on this topic, you are invited to visit my Web site.[19]

A Catholic Mystic on the Divine Seed

The seed of God is in us. Given an intelligent and hard-working farmer, it will thrive and grow up to God, whose seed it is; and accordingly its fruits will be god-nature. Pear seeds grow into pear trees, nut seeds into nut trees, and God seed into God.

—Meister Eckhart, German Christian mystic, ca. 1300

Letting Go of "For Adults Only" Religion

(This is a sample of the kind of write-up that can be used for ministry reflection in a small, intentional spiritual community within a congregation. The incident is imaginary, but the issue it raises is critical for a transforming congregation.)

Brief Background

I have been involved in the congregation for nine years and have held several leadership positions. All three of my children are in their teens and are less interested in being involved in the congregation than I would like.

The Situation

When my children were young, I taught in the church school on Sundays. But in recent years I have enjoyed focusing on the kind of interactions I am having with adults involved with me in congregational service projects (shared ministry) in the neighborhood. Also, congregational worship is very important in my life.

I find myself thinking about my children, though, bothered by their lack of interest and enthusiasm about participating in church. I can get them to attend, but their reactions are very different from mine.

As I remember the kinds of things we taught the children in church school in the earlier years, I wonder if the way we handled it has something to do with the kind of response they are now having.

There was that earlier period when so much of what we presented was information—stories about heroes of faith, moral teachings, and the like. Then we used those newer materials that focused more on discussion and the young people's own reactions and responses.

When I think of what we have accomplished recently in our congregation's move from adult education to adult spiritual development and the beneficial effect that has had, I wonder about the kids. Is there such a thing as children's spirituality? If so, how might our congregation help them in that? Our earlier curriculum material for the children was neatly organized by abstract historical and thematic considerations and it seemed removed from the children's real concerns. The newer material seems so loose that it carries a catch-as-catch-can feeling similar to that of our former adult education program.

But I wonder about personal and shared ministry and about spiritual formation for young people?

My Overall Thoughts and Feelings

I feel sad and a bit guilty when I consider the part I may have had in letting our congregation's youth down. I am glad for the challenge and uplift I get from my own experience in worship, and I want our kids and others in the congregation to have the same positive experiences in their own involvement in the congregation. I like our new focus on lay ministry and spiritual development for adults, but I wonder if there aren't ways for us to take these into what the congregation does with and for its young people.

The Focus for Our Reflection

What can I do to help our congregation apply its emphasis on spiritual formation and lay ministry in its work with young people, so that kids can be helped to find opportunities for ministry in their own lives and can be better nurtured in their spiritual development?

Suggestions for the Reader's Reflection and Discussion

- *After you have read through the full text of the conversation, go back and read it again, placing a question mark by anything that you wonder about. Put a star by anything that elicits a feeling in you.*
- *Jot down some notes identifying each question or feeling and what in your experience might give rise to the question or feeling. Spend some time thinking about your responses.*
- *Write (or discuss with others) your reactions to the following:*
  - *What themes am I noticing in my responses?*
  - *What do my responses tell me about myself?*
  - *What do these responses tell me about what is going on in my personal ministry?*
  - *What experiences, images, stories, or teachings from my spiritual roots come to mind in relation to this conversation and my reflection on it?*

Letting Go into Images

"My grandmother had told them to me—stories that kept wonder alive in me. . . . The stories were like kisses from my grandmother, and I lived them, because when I heard them my mind was nothing but pictures."

> — a comment by an unidentified Puerto Rican story-teller in a *New Yorker* magazine report on a storytelling festival in Central Park[1]

Letting Go Inwardly—An Exercise

Spend some time alone. You will need at least an uninterrupted half hour.

Notice what's on your mind, but take whatever arises there and gently lift it aside. Set them all down where you can retrieve them later. Quiet down. Breathe deeply. Say a prayer for inward peace.

When you are ready, look around in there. See what you notice.

Look to see if you can find an image for your spirit, for your spiritual life. What comes up for you as a metaphor for your spirit?

Spend some time letting it be there, exploring it, paying attention to its shape, its color, its movement, its feel.

(Before you turn the page,
give yourself all the time you need
to let an image come.)

Letting Go Inwardly—An Exercise Continues 1

(See previous page.)

If no image appeared, pay attention. That happens for some people and is also an appropriate response. In some mystical traditions emptiness itself is an image. It signifies richness of possibility. If your image is "nothing," let "nothing" be there.

Now look again.

Look to see if you can find an image for your spirit, for your spiritual life. Another image. What comes up for you as a metaphor for your spirit? Spend some time letting it be there.

Letting Go Inwardly—An Exercise Continues 2

(See previous pages.)

Look again. One final time.

Look to see if you can find a third image for your spirit, for your spiritual life. What comes up for you as another metaphor for your spirit? Spend some time letting it be there. Explore it. Pay attention to its shape. Its color, sound, size, smell.

When you have a full sense of this image, bring the other two back to your attention.

Now see if you can combine them—all three together into one image, if possible. Is there a story that puts them together? A larger encompassing image?

They do belong together in you. How do they fit together? What does that fit tell you? What does it have to do with your life these days? What does it have to do with themes in your life over the years?

Is there something you might want to do with this? Think of someone with whom you would be willing to share your images.

Some people take delight in conjuring up one or more of these images from time to time. They find that the images bring comfort or are a reminder of deeper currents and underlying connections.

The Artist Philip Guston on Letting Go

When you're in the studio painting, there are a lot of people in there
with you. Your teachers, friends, painters from history, critics . . .
and one by one, if you're really painting, they walk out. And if you're
really painting, you walk out.

—From a talk between artists Philip Guston and Audrey Flack[2]

Jesus on Letting Go

It is to your advantage that I go away, for if I do not go away, the
Advocate will not come to you; but if I go, I will send him to you.
(John 16:7)

CHAPTER 4

From Diversity to Engagement

Creative Interchange

I was 19 years old, studying chemical engineering, and not enjoying my studies very much, but doing well enough. Even though I had thrown out most of the traditional symbols of religion in an adolescent clearing of the conceptual deck, I was interested in religion and philosophy. Besides, I had just fallen in love. The relationship would be brief, but it was profoundly different from earlier experience. We interacted with a degree of authenticity I had not known before. We spoke to one another from our original experience of how things seemed and felt. We shared genuine thoughts, not what we guessed we were expected to say.

This was a new experience for me—a new level of integrity and honesty of interchange. That was in Boston in the winter of 1960.

At the time this was happening, I was involved in a church-sponsored group for college students. At one of the meetings I heard that an influential and innovative philosopher of religion was coming to town to speak. He was Henry Nelson Wieman, Whiteheadian process thinker and early representative of the naturalistic, empiricist 'Chicago School' theological outlook. He was to deliver several speeches around Boston during a two- or three-day period. I attended the first one and something significant fell into place for me. I didn't yet know what.

Trying to identify it, I followed him around and heard him speak several times during his days in the area. I was intrigued with his understanding of religion.

Across cultures, he said, this is *the* religious question: "What transforms us as we cannot transform ourselves, to save us from our self-destructive tendencies and to bring us to the highest good of which we are capable?"

Wieman said that the answer to this question in most of the great religions is usually: "God. God transforms us."

Then, being quintessentially American in his thinking, he said, "I am an empiricist. I need to be able to experience this myself or it can mean nothing to me. So I ask, where in our experience is this that transforms people as they cannot transform themselves?" And he answered, "It is found best in a certain kind of interaction between people, a certain quality of conversation." He was speaking, I would later learn, of what Jewish theologian Martin Buber had called an "I-Thou" relationship.[1] Lowell Streiker, an interpreter of Buber's work, explains the significance of that unusual, hyphenated word. "There are not two worlds of experience, the sacred and the profane," Buber taught. Rather there is one world and two possible responses to it. "We may use, enjoy, manipulate, experience, analyze and know the world. Or beyond this, we may regard the same world of the everyday as the context of our relationship to God." When we thus hallow the world, we "bind [ourself] to God in each act by responding completely, unaffectedly, openly with the wholeness of [our] being to the concrete circumstances of [our] life."[2] When we interact with another in genuine reciprocity and mutuality, communication becomes communion and we are experiencing "life in God."

Wieman wrote in *Man's Ultimate Commitment*, a book I was soon to read, that our commitment to that

Reflect on some of the most important conversations you have had with another. What stands out? What happened? What difference did the conversations make for you? For the other person?

kind of communication is the *only* way to avoid what he referred to as "spiritual death." Spiritual death, he said, is "failure to live with the vivid qualities of original experience, with the full exercise of personal resources . . . with realization of one's constructive potentialities and with a deep sense of the worthwhileness of life."[3] Only through that special committed kind of communication with other people can such spiritual death be avoided. His name for that way of relating is *creative interchange*. He carefully spells out its meaning. It is different from "the clichés, the stale conventions, and the automatic reactions"[4] we tend to use in everyday casual interaction. These forms of interaction have their appropriate place in human experience, but they are not the transformational communication Wieman is attempting to identify.

Creative interchange requires that both people listen generously and receptively to the other, intending to gain "an appreciative understanding of the original experience" of the other and working to integrate the other's experience so it "becomes a part of one's own original experience." This involves acquiring information from the other, but there is also the exchange of "appreciations, sentiments, hopes, fears, memories, regrets, aspirations, joys, sorrows, hates, loves, pieties, and other features of that vast complexity which makes up the total experience of every human being."[5]

With whom and in which settings do you share these aspects of your experience? Are there some of these you never share?

Wieman emphasizes that this kind of interaction will not happen automatically but requires personal commitment. Transformational communication is, thus, a spiritual discipline. It is a unique form of spiritual discipline because one can choose alone to enter into it, but one cannot engage in it as a solitary exercise. It requires a genuine and open engagement with another.

To the degree that a person commits to this kind of engagement, Wieman says, two profound things happen. The person experiences both a deepening sense of self and the generation and increase of love.

The love of which Wieman speaks involves much more than a sentimental feeling of connection. He means love as "an appreciative understanding and cherishing" of another, as "a recognition of the unknown and unsearched depth of subjectivity" in the other, and as "deference and deep concern for this hidden subjectivity" that resides in every human person.[6]

Wieman is saying that what creates, sustains, and renews us is God, and that God is primarily known in generous, receptive engagement with others. This is close to the biblical saying "God is love." It involves a religious sense of the mystery and greatness of persons and the expectation that sacred energies will be released when people engage authentically and receptively with one another.

What does this phrase mean to you: "God is love"?

In identifying this kind of communication as God, Wieman spoke more starkly than many would. He was interested in being rigorous, even minimalist, in his theological statements. He knew that religious folk tend to talk in terms of powers residing in other realms. That kind of talk, he felt, misdirected people's attention, distracted them from real experience of the divine, and discouraged them from committing themselves to sharing, in their own unique ways, in God's work. He insisted that, beneath all the words, we should focus our attention on the places where we meet, the interactions in which we engage, and the daily opportunities and challenges we face—for these, in fact, are the occasions when we can witness and participate in the creative, sustaining, transformative work of the divine. Through creative interchange, human beings can be together in a way that advances the work of creation. Creative interchange is human beings intentionally participating in the life and work of God.

There I was in Boston, 19 years old, experiencing in my relationship with a young woman a depth of communication I had not experienced before, and here was a religious thinker saying that what I was experiencing was the highest, that it was what religion was all about and what the church existed to promote. What was I to do with all this?

Within a few months of hearing Wieman speak, I decided to discontinue studying chemical engineering and began studying to become a minister of such a transformational religion.

Structured for Conflict?

Six years later I was ordained. For more than three decades since then, I have almost always enjoyed my work in congregations, and even during difficult times I have felt myself challenged and growing in it. But early in my ministry I felt a vague disappointment. Busy and involved in the work at hand, I did not let my uneasiness come fully into my awareness. Probably I didn't want to notice that the day-to-day life of the congregation held little of the quality of interaction Wieman had said religion is for, and what I had thought congregational life would be about. Committees, coffee hours, classes, fund raising, governance concerns, even support groups—these were not designed to permit or to encourage the kind of spiritual growth or shared ministry I thought the work had promised.

Have you experienced spiritually significant or ministry-related moments in the everyday activities of your congregation? When? What was different about those moments? What difference did they make for you?

Maybe I ought to settle for those kinds of groups and interactions, I thought, and give up my adolescent sense of transformational possibility. But at its worst, congregational life can generate hurtful interactions, pettiness, gossip, jealousy, and power grabs, and it can bring out a mean-spiritedness that I didn't want to settle for. People carry with them into congregational life what they know about how to be in relationship, about how to feel significant, and how to function in groups. Sometimes what they know and bring is disappointingly inadequate. I knew I couldn't be content to settle for that.

There were moments, I admit, when I felt a twinge of failure and of shame because I was the lead minister of a congregation in which some bickering or other unwholesome sort of interaction had been occurring. I felt responsible, too, for the fact that we were not really developing ways to put into practice the kind of interaction Wieman had named in my youth. But I knew the shortcomings of congregational life couldn't simply be my fault or the responsibility of any one or two congregation leaders.

Perhaps, I thought, the bickering and unpleasantness that sometimes occurs can be understood as "simply human nature." (That's just the way people are; don't expect so much.) But I soon saw that explaining congregational upset that way—as simply human nature—isn't the mature, tough-minded theological assessment it may at first appear to be. Often it is merely another way to avoid looking squarely at the way the congregation is structured.

Have you ever been stunned or disappointed when "human nature" or personality conflicts at their worst appeared in the congregation? What happened? How did you feel? What did you do?

So then I thought that maybe congregational upset isn't a mere outcropping of human nature but occurs during one of those "bad years" that hits from time to time, bringing an unfortunate mix of "difficult" personalities into leadership positions at the same time. Maybe. But I came more and more to believe that the unwholesomeness which occurs in congregations is a consequence of the way congregations are structured and organized. At least it was a possibility worth exploring. The other views were tantamount to merely throwing up one's hands in despair. That is not "letting go." That would be giving up.

An example of how these various possible explanations play out in congregations might be helpful. There is a common, biting, "backstage" saying among church leaders: "When Lucifer was ejected from heaven, he landed in the choir." When that is said, people tend to react in one of two ways: either they laugh in recognition, then follow their laughter with a signal that one shouldn't say such a "naughty" thing, or they are outraged that such a terrible thing could be thought. Yet those who spend much time near congregations know that the outrageous saying is a way of acknowledging the common tension between the "music department" and other parts of the congregation.

We may try to understand this tension as merely the inevitable clash of clergy personalities with the personalities of musicians. They clash; congregational tensions result; nothing can be done about "human nature;" nothing can be done about the ways any two particular people antagonize each other.

There is the other alternative, however. It is the structural explanation: to assume that such tensions result when an important ministry within the congregation is not fully acknowledged as a ministry. What if people who devotedly participate in rehearsals and make their best efforts toward a worshipful sound week after week are not adequately and appropriately incorporated into the planning, funding, evaluation, and recognition processes of the congregation's overall plan of ministry? What if these people are not, therefore, full participants in and "owners" of the ministry plan? Might not that situation almost inevitably generate conflict?

What change in the way a meeting or a group was organized made a difference in the quality of the interactions that took place afterwards?

Resolution is more likely to come about when people go beyond the common explanations ("the clergyman's fault," "simply human nature," or "difficult personalities") and look for the diagnosis of the trouble in considerations of vision, shared mission, the availability of spiritual development resources, and the need to find better ways to share, evaluate, and celebrate the congregation's ministry. It is usually the case that carefully considered and widely adopted–not *imposed*–changes in the congregation's visioning and decision-making processes help people come together wholesomely again.

Tolerating Each Other

When I decided to become a parish minister, I had supposed that actual congregations would provide the fertile environment in which the divine seed in people would flourish. The cultivation of potential would happen through genuine, mutual conversation. Congregational activities would be designed to encourage and evoke that kind of creative, transformational, sustaining engagement.

Instead I learned there is always a strong pull into institution-maintenance work, into maneuvering for position and power, into "educational" distractions and entertainments. Instead of spirit-enhancing engagement with one another, people are drawn into busyness or choose to tolerate the diversity of people in the congregation from the distance of interpersonal neutrality.

Put positively, tolerance means that if you want to participate in a congregation, for instance, you can do that without first having to "get your beliefs on straight." You will not be subjected to that form of spiritual abuse people experience when pushed to believe or declare something not true to their experience. You will not be required to look, dress, think, feel, speak, or live like the majority of people in the congregation because, as it is said, the congregation "welcomes diversity . . . regardless of ethnicity, race, preferences, gender, and so on."

How does the phrase "spiritual abuse" fit with your experience in congregations? In relationships? At work?

But the negative side of the neutrality, which some congregations call "tolerance of diversity," is the fact that this neutrality is merely a polite cordiality that is safe but not lively or challenging. Ultimately it is not even really safe; it is harmful. Michael Cowan and Bernard Lee see this as "a collusion in denial."[7]

In their book *Conversation, Risk and Conversion*, these Catholic theologians suggest that barrenness develops when a congregation doesn't seem a safe place for genuine and vulnerable interaction and when people are unwilling to accept the discipline required in order to play by the rules of what Michael Cowan calls "the sacred game of conversation."[8]

David Tracy, Roman Catholic theologian at the University of Chicago Divinity School, spells out the rules of the game of conversation:

> Conversation is a game with some hard rules: say only what you mean; say it as accurately as you can; listen to and respect what the other says, however different or other; be willing to correct or defend your opinions if challenged by the conversation partner; be willing to argue if necessary, to confront if demanded, to endure necessary conflict, to change your mind if the evidence suggests it.[9]

In many congregations the words "tolerance," "inclusiveness," "diversity," "pluralism," "politeness," and "civility" can be virtuous-sounding names for an environment in which people play it safe in uncreative non-engagement, where people refuse to share their own experiences about significant concerns or to engage seriously and receptively with the experiences of another.

Cowan and Lee write that a prime reason we avoid engagement is that it may lead to the need to change.

> Receptivity to otherness in interpersonal conversation requires a willingness to have our interpretation of life put at risk. Others may be carrying a message that will force us into the painful realization that something else might, and perhaps should, be the case with our life.[10]

When has the word "diversity" been applied to an interaction you have participated in or witnessed? Were the participants vibrantly engaged with one another? If so (or if not) what difference did it make for you or others?

Unfortunately, avoiding that risk in an effort to keep safe might also cut us off from the possibility that the other will deeply affirm us or that mutual challenge might occur that would bring about a significant growth in us, in the other person, and in the community.

Beyond Tolerance of Diversity to Engagement

Cowan and Lee are engaged in an extensive study of small Christian communities. They have watched some of these communities develop a rare level of engaged conversation.[11] The quality they have fostered and witnessed there demonstrates anew to me that the "creative interchange" Wieman advocated can and does take place, at least occasionally, in religious settings. As these theologians understand it, people choose intentionally to participate in the life and work of God when they work to deepen their interaction with one another in their personal settings and in the institutions and associations of the wider community. Such engagement advances the work of creation.

One of the fundamental tenets of the American dream is the high value put on interaction among differing people. This vision works more readily in ritual and ceremony or in large civic gatherings than it does in practical interactions in congregations or in local neighborhoods or in community associations and institutions. We feel its power at the opening of a sports event when we stand in the stadium with friends and strangers to sing the national anthem. A sense of it comes to us when we kneel with others at the communion railing. It touches us when we pray together in large interracial or interfaith gatherings. In the culture of America, in congregations, in stories and teachings drawn from the Bible, we hear this ideal articulated in many ways again and again: *e pluribus unum*—strangers from different places can find ways to function together, to work as a unit, to experience union amidst differences.

The underlying American affirmation is not only that this is possible, but that it is desirable, that new qualities will emerge into the very scheme of things when such engagement takes place among diverse individuals. A secular expression of this hope of creativity arising from pluralism appears in a memorable passage written in 1943 by Learned Hand, distinguished judge of the United States federal court.

> Right conclusions are more likely to be gathered out of a multitude of tongues than through any kind of authoritative selection. To many this is, and will always be, folly; but we have staked upon it our all.[12]

While good emerging from multiplicity is in some unique ways a fundamentally American ideal, it has deep religious roots in the powerful and persistent idea of a God of *all* nations, the one source of the heavens, the earth and *all* the powers therein, *all* creatures great and small. Early in the life of the new nation, Ralph Waldo Emerson wrote, "God is Unity, but always works in variety."[13]

In his book *The Company of Strangers*, Parker Palmer reminds us that in biblical stories of faith, the stranger is a central figure. He says there is good reason for that centrality. "The religious quest, the spiritual pilgrimage, is always taking us into new lands where we are strange to others and they are strange to us. Faith is a venture into the unknown, into the realms of mystery, away from the safe and comfortable and secure."[14] He challenges the ideal of a congregation as a gathering of friendly people, saying it ought to be a place where we are sure to encounter a stranger. He reminds us of the ancient custom of welcome and hospitality to strangers: "Do not neglect to show hospitality to strangers, for by doing that some have entertained angels without knowing it." (Heb. 13:2)

Describe an encounter with a stranger that was the source of blessing for you. For the stranger.

In addition, the ideal of the grace-filled encounter with the stranger is disclosed in the image of Jesus as one who came eating and drinking, sitting at the table and interacting with all comers—Jesus, the one who declared that "eating and living together without any distinctions, differences, discriminations, or hierarchies"[15] is a sign of the kingdom hidden, yet potential in the present time, and coming in the future.

The image of the creative possibilities that can emerge from engagement with the other who is different is carried in the driving images of the Christian vision and in those of other religions, in the great ideals of the American experiment, and in the revitalization of American spirituality that arose after the Revolutionary War in the image of the divine seed present in all people. We know, sadly, how seldom these visions are made actual in the real world of human interaction and association. Yet the image stands as call for transformation in American institutional life and, to this book's point, a call to transformed congregational life.

The central dimension of a transformed congregation in the American cultural milieu will be the encouragement of creative interchange between people. This change will require that we dismantle some of those organizational committees and that we change certain of our customary ways of gathering (even, perhaps, the almost universal after-worship coffee hour) in order to permit a richer quality of interaction within the congregation. Only after we disrupt such familiar practices can we begin to treat one another in new and better ways. The present structure of congregational organizations and gatherings significantly limits how we engage with one another. We must be willing to question and reinvent those practices, because they are the primary resources available to our religious communities by which to cultivate the divine seed in people, encouraging it to flower in spiritual deepening and to bear fruit in personal and shared ministry in the world.

How much change and disruption do you think your congregation could tolerate? In what ways might this be a good time to begin making changes? Why might this be the wrong time?

Mutuality

Such concerns for change moved leaders in the Minnesota congregation to initiate a search for ways to integrate spiritual development and ministry considerations into all sorts of congregational activities. How, they asked, can we modify the way these tasks are carried out so people can engage in the work, reflect upon it, share with others about it, and thus encounter it not merely as a task, but also as an occasion for growth? They envisioned dealing with many kinds of work in this new way: social action outreach into the neighborhood of the church and beyond, the work of church groups and task forces, as well as the personal ministries of congregants—in their homes with their families, at work, and in their community involvements.

In the course of their search for a new approach, they found BeFriender Ministry at the University of St. Thomas in St. Paul.[16] The BeFriender program trains laypeople in offering pastoral care to their fellow parishioners and welcomes the congregation's leaders into the training. Participants learn the program's powerful method of encouraging "situated learning" within a congregation through reflecting together on their experiences of carrying out their ministry. The Minnesota congregation leaders were encouraged by the program's trainers as they adapted and applied what they learned from the Befriender program to several areas of their congregation's practice, including even the work of the congregation's staff.

An outline of the ministry reflection process will be given here, but readers should know this description connects to participants' actual experience in the way a choreographer's score connects to the ensemble's actual performance of the dance. It bears the same abstract relationship a playwright's manuscript does to the action taking place up on stage on opening night. As a person familiar with the ministry reflection process commented, "For some reason, talking about this process never sounds as engaging and life-giving as I know it is."

Participants form into groups of 8 to 12 people who commit to learning the method and practicing it twice each month for about an hour and a half each session. One member serves as facilitator as another presents a brief written case report or a verbatim write-up of a ministry-related situation. The presenter identifies a single focus question for the session. Examples of focus questions are:

How would you answer these questions?

- "How can I better respond when dealing with a person who uses her time with me to complain about the way the church raises money?"
- "How can I create an animated worship experience that is relevant to the real life concerns of children?"
- "How can I engage newcomers within our congregation so they feel welcomed?"

People ask clarifying questions that arise as they prepare to focus their energies on the area of the presenter's concern. When people are clear about the presenter's focus, the facilitator monitors a 20-minute conversation conducted in a highly structured format. Each person in the group may speak, but no advice is to be given to the presenter. Speakers are to share both *feelings and thoughts* that arise within them in response to the ministry situation presented. ("Your experience in that office makes me feel discouraged, the way I felt years ago when my aunt had her driver's license suspended." "A sadness came over me as you spoke, because I was recalling how it used to be when my brothers, sisters, and I all went home for Christmas.")

After each of these sharings, the original presenter reflects what the person just said—in both its emotive and cognitive dimensions. This attempt at accurate understanding continues until the speaker is satisfied that the listener understands what was meant.

That 20 minutes of interaction is followed by 5 minutes of shared group silence during which each member reflects privately on what happened during the previous interchange: what themes emerged, what inner stirrings occurred, what connections were made to issues they have encountered in their own lives and ministries. During this period some people experience a rush of insights about themselves or about new approaches they can take in their own ministries. Most important is that these "suggestions" come from within and are thus the person's own. Given the way most people function, suggestions that arise this way are more likely to be incorporated into the person's future practice than are suggestions imposed by somebody else.

After the shared silence there is a period in which each group member is invited to share insights or observations that apply to his or her own ministry. The process is not meant to address the presenter's situation or even the presenter's original focus question. Each group member is thus encouraged to take responsibility for his or her own learning. Usually an amazing array of things is shared, illustrating the richness of gifts present in the people involved, and in their similarities and their differences.

Tell of a time when, in a conversation or some other situation, you have had a "flash of the spirit" that opened something important for you.

Then, after another period of silence shared together, people are invited to tell of any faith-related impulses or insights related to the conversation's focus that may have arisen during the silence or the interaction, such as religious themes, insights, biblical passages, or spiritual nudges. This too is often rich beyond expectation: people sharing fragments of poetry, stories from various religious traditions, remembrances of works of art, themes from pieces of music, stirrings of the spirit.

My description conveys little of the richness that emerges during the interaction. People in these groups share in the struggle to say what they really mean, and it becomes obvious to all how difficult that sometimes can be. One group developed a "feelings list" because so many people in this culture need help finding words for their emotional life. But people laugh at times and they weep, and a deep feeling of connectedness emerges within the group. People who participate in this process over time tell of an im-provement—sometimes a dramatic improvement—in their ability to express themselves and to listen with understanding to others. They report that these changes make a difference not only during the meetings them-selves, but later on at work and at home—with their coworkers, their spouses, their children, their parents, and others. Personal transformations of this kind are clearly part of the mission of congregational life in action.

When I first participated in the training, I sensed the enrichment this process might bring to a congrega-tion. In addition, the ministry reflection process had a familiar ring. Somewhere in its origins, I guessed, would be found the influence of Henry Nelson Wieman. I read a book that gave me some of the background of the reflection process. The book was *Dangerous Memories: House Churches and Our American Story*, which had been written in the mid-1980s by Bernard Lee and Michael Cowan. Eventually I spoke with Cowan, a theologian trained in psychology and group work who now teaches pastoral theology at Loyola University in New Orleans. I learned that he was the primary resource in the development of the BeFriender Ministry Program's reflection model.

Cowan had been influenced by his work with Catholic process/empiricist theologian Bernard Lee. Lee had been a student of one of my teachers, Chi-cago School theologian Bernard Loomer. And Loomer had studied with Wieman. The influence is clear.

With this discovery, the connection had come full circle, and I felt that I had come home. An idea that I had first heard expressed by an innovative philosopher of religion in the early 1960s lay largely dormant until Roman Catholics, who were influenced by the same idea, began to put it into practice in enhancing lay ministry in small Christian communities. Leaders in the Minnesota congregation, moving outside their denominational boundaries to the Catholics, found for themselves a method that had at its core the very same creative interchange that I had almost despaired of introducing into congregational life. What those leaders found was most congenial to their congregation's faith perspective and it helped inspire them to begin structuring methods of spiritual formation and shared ministry into the very processes of congregational life.

This method for doing congregational work (and many other kinds of work as well) is an interpersonal spiritual discipline now named *mutuality*. Its key underlying elements as presented in the BeFriender program[17] are these:

- Each person orders events in his or her life by interpreting them. For each of us, the overall picture of how life works, which each puts together continuously through interpretations, can be called the *assumptive world*.
- Our assumptive world makes possible and limits our interpretation of any event, and any particular interpretation, in turn, affects our assumptive world.
- In order to relate to another in an enriching and creative way, we must acknowledge and connect with that person's assumptive world.
- We may or may not agree with another's assumptive world, but we must strive to understand it and must affirm the other's right to hold it.
- Coming in touch with another's assumptive world affects our own. Ours may be altered or it may be confirmed in new ways.

List two major elements of your own assumptive world and an important relationship in which you had to work on differences related to one or both of these assumptions.

- Mutuality cannot coexist with control, manipulation, isolation, or alienation.
- Mutuality demands concrete, behavioral, learnable skills (naming feelings, listening appreciatively to the other, paraphrasing what others say, giving specific feedback). This requires and helps deepen an attitude of respect and reverence for life stories, our own and those of others. Mutuality is not merely a technique or an attitude. It is an interpersonal, spiritual discipline that requires and cultivates self-restraint, receptivity, generosity, courage, honesty, expectancy, and trust.

This ministry-reflection process provides a way to evoke creative interchange within a group setting, among friends, colleagues, and strangers. As an interpersonal spiritual discipline, it can contribute to the spiritual formation of both speaker and listener. The spiritual deepening that emerges from the give-and-take of the dialogue comes in the form of a greatly enriched, more expansive outlook. Cowan's expression of the process, reproduced in the BeFriender's training manual, incorporates Loomer's outlook and some of his language, and shows how dialogic give-and-take can affect the participants' spiritual orientation:

- Every act of authentic self-disclosure makes one person's story a gift to the becoming of another.
- Every act of genuine understanding of another's story enhances the size of the listener's spirit.
- Every act of responsible challenge in the spirit of understanding is an invitation to an increase in stature.
- Every act of non-defensive exploration in response to challenge reflects a commitment to a life of larger dimensions.[18]

When have you grown as the result of genuinely understanding another's story?

I have practiced and taught this method of mutuality in a number of settings and I have never stopped being amazed by the effect it has on people when they engage with one another in this way. It is applicable in a great variety of contexts inside and outside congregational life.

Other Ways of Reflecting Together

In my initial enthusiasm about this discovery, I thought we had hit upon a reflection process that would apply in every aspect of congregational life. For various reasons, this didn't turn out to be true. The process requires a greater commitment of time in training and monthly practice than some people and some groups wanted to invest. In addition, some individuals—a surprisingly small number—complained that the disciplined alternation of speaking, listening, and reflecting felt artificial and confining. But most people reported reactions more like this one spoken by the congregation's head custodian and facilities manager, Dennis Kreuser (who was not a congregation member) as he reflected on one of these groups that had been formed within the church staff.

> I was strongly against a staff reflection process at first; after all, this was my job, not group therapy. But I can say that our staff's [process] has been a transformative experience for me. In my own life, with my parents and with my kids, I've noticed how often my ideas are in the way of really listening to them. We're always so quick to form opinions about what's being said, or to think we know what someone else means. As much as I do what I think is good for my kids, I've learned that if I don't help them learn and grow up their own way, not mine, I'm not doing them much good. In the workplace, coworkers here have developed a trust that goes beyond just working together, but

is different than a friendship. Getting together not to solve a problem or accomplish something, but to share experiences and emotions, has helped me notice how inadequately I've been listening to people. These conversations have been times when I've witnessed people expressing their spirituality and their deeper values, and during these conversations, different definitions of spirituality don't get in the way."[19]

That kind of reaction was not universal, but widespread. We began doing research to see what additional methods of reflection might be available for groups and meetings in which the primary ministry reflection model would not be used.

Walter Wink's method of bible study referred to in chapter 3 is another example of a disciplined approach to conversation that often results in stunning personal insights that people carry with them into other parts of their lives.

Some of the other valuable sources of models of spiritual deepening through small-group reflection are noted here. Most of the exploration for such methods seems to be taking place outside the church in our day. Many work teams in a secular setting are experimenting with shared vision, innovative methods of reflecting on their work, and team learning. While these teams seldom have an acknowledged theological dimension, increasingly they are aware of their spiritual basis, and leaders of congregations will find that some of the approaches could be adapted for congregational life. As a starting place, one useful source that summarizes a number of these methods of reflective practice is *The Fifth Discipline Fieldbook: Strategies and Tools for Building a Learning Organization*[20] by Peter Senge of the Massachusetts Institute of Technology Learning Center and his associates.

Another important contribution is made in the work

of educator Donald A Schön, also of the Massachusetts Institute of Technology, in exploring the diminishment that took place in the closing decades of the 20th century in the reputation of professionalism.

The conventional model sees a professional as a person who enters a situation, diagnoses a problem, and then applies technical skills to solve the problem. Both the general public and some professionals, however, have been noticing the limitations of this model. For some time they have seen that there are situations too complex, too ambiguous, and too rapidly changing to be convincingly diagnosed this way. They have sensed, also, the resourcefulness of some of the participants in the situation besides the one who has been designated "professional."

What other resources related to teams and improvement of communication can you share?

In two important books on "the reflective practitioner," Schön relates an emerging alternative view, which describes a professional as one who is skilled at reflection-in-action[21] and which details innovations he has studied in training professionals[22] in the "core of artistry" that is needed in competent contemporary professional practice. In *Educating the Reflective Practitioner: Toward a New Design for Teaching and Learning in the Professions*, he writes:

> In the terrain of professional practice, applied science and research-based technique occupy a critically important though limited territory, bounded on several sides by artistry. There are an art of problem framing, an art of implementation, and an art of improvisation—all necessary to mediate the use in practice of applied science and technique.[23]

Schön's work helps us better understand the cultural setting of the professions in our day. This can lead those interested in congregational life to a more adequate perception of issues of ministry. These books tell of specific innovative experiments in the training of certain professionals (psychoanalysts, architects, managers, counselors, physicians, engineers, musical performers) that seminaries will find useful in the training of clergy and that clergy will find useful as they work in congregations training people for lay ministry.

In the Minnesota congregation we experimented with ways to change the focus and tone of committees from the customary task-only agenda into something richer. Abandoning the nondescript name "committee" helped. Thereafter people had to reflect about what they would name their group. If it's not a committee, then what is it? What is its purpose? Is it a task force? A ministry team? These two names were adopted by a number of groups.

Make a list of all the different names used for types of groups in your congregation. Do the names convey important information about what the groups are for?

The change of name signified a change in identity and a move more deeply into living the congregation's mission and its intended outcomes. We applied the outcomes matrix and again it helped us see more clearly the development that was called for next. We noticed that it had more elements than the four poles and the four quadrants we had recognized earlier. Now we focused on the horizontal and vertical axes, wondering what they might signify. We noticed that the horizontal axis connected the INWARD outcome (spiritual deepening) with the OUTWARD (ministry, action in the world). When we considered these two outcomes as interconnected, we were able to name the horizontal axis: *Reflection-in-Action* or *Reflective Practice* (fig. 4).

Similarly, we began to see the connection between the INDIVIDUALITY and the COMMUNITY outcomes. Considered together, these two suggest that people become most fully themselves when they engage in community with others, and communities are fulfilled when individuals and clusters of individuals interact. The vertical axis shows this by naming authentic interaction between individuals in community: *Mutuality*.

So at last we understood the outcomes in a way that brought them all together. Early in our work with

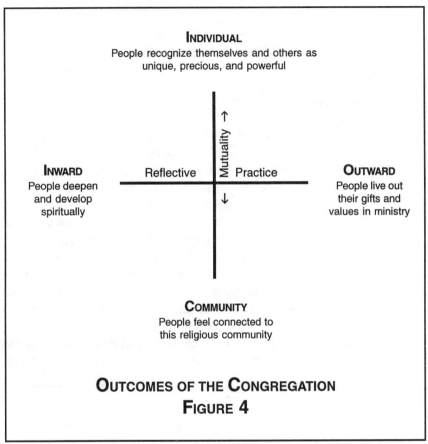

OUTCOMES OF THE CONGREGATION
FIGURE 4

the matrix somebody had asked, "What is represented by that center point where the axes meet?" Now we could answer and could, thus, summarize a congregation's mission and outcomes all in one breath:

In what ways do you agree with this statement? What improvements would you make?

People engaged with others in authentic and respectful sharing of thoughts and feelings about experiences in their life's ministry can expect to come to a new level of spirit and a new degree of effectiveness in action.

With this new sense of the integration of the outcomes, we worked to develop ways in which task groups and ministry teams not using the primary Ministry Reflection model could experience some of what the groups using it were experiencing. One key way we did this was to design a process by which these more casual groups could engage in mutuality and reflective practice, both at once.

In this process, leaders among the laity and the staff carefully crafted questions and queries that were then used as the opening focus for the group's meeting. As much as one-third of the group's meeting time was spent in the lively activity of sharing responses to these reflective questions. Over time this significantly enriched the tone of the church's meetings.

The gatherings took on a more appropriate "feel of church" and became more spiritually alive, especially when the reflective questions were framed to fit metaphorically with the literal "business" that the meeting was called to transact—in ways some of the following examples will illustrate:

Try responding to each of the italicized directives and questions that appear in the remainder of this section.

In a gathering of eight people whose team assignment was to shape a process to determine the feasible overall dollar goal for an upcoming capital fund drive, the first 40 minutes were spent in sharing personal responses to the query: *Tell of a time in your life when something not feasible—a time when the "impossible"—happened.* In the course of the sharing, one member told about an utterly unexpected recovery from his crippling childhood disease, another about working through her stammering and stage fright into skilled public speaking. One told of four self-motivated seven-year-old girls holding a sidewalk bake sale and raising over $250 to send off for flood relief.

At one of its weekly meetings, the staff team shared responses to this: *Think about your personal talents and gifts. Which one do you feel best about today? Why? If there were one additional gift you could acquire immediately, with no effort, what would it be?*

On one of the first blustery November mornings, staff members were invited to explore and share: *What part of you is in hibernation these days?*

The congregation's trustees began the first meeting of the new church year taking as their focus: *Come prepared to share a concrete instance, story, or experience in which being a trustee was, for you, a ministry. Or share a specific example of how some non-board experience has been for you a ministry.*

At a board meeting in which the professional auditor from outside the congregation was to give her annual report on her firm's review of the church's financial records, the trustees viewed a portion of Bill Moyers' PBS video *Amazing Grace*. They then shared their responses to the following assignment that had been sent out with the meeting's agenda:

> In business, audits are performed by internal or external accountants to examine and authenticate an organization's accounts. John Newton, author and composer of the song "Amazing Grace," began an "audit" of his life while in peril in a storm at sea. *Come prepared to share a story from your life in which an external or internal event presented you with the impetus to begin an audit of some part of your life. It could be a comment*

*made to you by another person or an event
that caused you to take stock of your outlook.*

After some 40 minutes of sharing responses with one
another, they invited the auditor into the room so they
could hear her report. With their earlier sharing as background, the word "audit" now carried a new tone, a
set of meanings that provided a rich setting for the
literal business at hand.

As the annual canvass for operating expenses was
gearing up, a gathering of canvass leaders was asked:
*When did the generous act of another make an
important difference in your life?*

A separate group of canvass leaders gathered to
determine the dollar "ask" amount for each congregational household. They spent the first 40 minutes of
their meeting responding to these directives: *Recall a
time when somebody asked you for something specific and the request got in the way of your giving
it. Recall a time when a specific request helped you
decide to give generously.*

Such questions fanned out through the various
groups and began to influence the general tone of the
congregation's work. The operational and governance
tasks were being handled, but now the tasks were less
dominating–and sometimes felt less ominous–because
they were being treated more lightly and less literally
and were being used as a way of opening participants
beyond the business into issues and energies related to
character, attitude, and ministry. The work was
done–but in an unconventional way, far less anxiously,
more richly and efficiently than before.

In the life of the congregation, the words of the
poet took on new and vivid meaning: "We walk through
forests of physical things that are also spiritual things
that look upon us with affectionate looks."[24]

A Call Forward

This new vision sees a congregation as a center for spiritual development and for the ministry of the laity. It is a "greenhouse" for ongoing spiritual formation, requiring a radical shift in congregational dynamics. It brings people from diversity and separateness into engaged interchange with one another's personally lived experience. The sharing results in a deepening sense of community and a new sense of richness in people's relationships. It energizes them to express their gifts and values in ministry in personal relationships, in their work, and in their community involvement.

This book tells of a mere beginning, made up of fits and starts. It tells of sifting and sorting, of accidental insights, of surprising connections, of disappointments and remarkable achievements. The experiment is a fragile beginning and is anything but complete. I have no idea whether what was attained in one congregation I led with others for a time will continue on under new leadership in new circumstances. (This is another sense of "letting go.")

My hope is that other congregations, other leaders, laity and clergy, will find encouragement and inspiration in what is written here. There are possibilities far beyond what we have yet seen, but if the work is to be done, if the new discoveries are to be made, if new ways of congregational life are to be shaped, we are the ones who are called to do it.

The emerging congregation I envision provides a powerful environment—physical and communal—to nurture a richer way of being so that people have a deeper sense of meaning and are drawn by a call into greater service. In such a congregation people will sense their own worth deep down and will enjoy the privilege of being alive in a reality they experience with awe. They will feel the worth of others. They will use opportunities to develop and to express their gifts and values. They will see their life and its challenges as the arena in which to live out those gifts and values—alone in personal ministry and with others in shared ministry—for the glory of self-expression, for the service of humanity, for the enrichment of the world, and for the greater glory of God.

What resources do you see in your congregation that could help things begin to move forward? How would you address the resistance that will arise?

Helping to shape such congregations will require dramatic changes that are not likely to be widely acclaimed, at least not for some time to come. There will be great initial resistance because it is in the nature of systems to find ever-new means for preventing and undoing change. However, the vision has now been made clear. It is the vision of a congregation as a community of spiritually deepening individuals engaging in personal and shared ministry.

A call for such congregations is sounding. It sounds from the creatures of a troubled planet, from deep in the life of the spirit, from high moments in the history of religions—Christian and others. It sounds in the potential we know is waiting within ourselves and in others and from the energies that people engaged in shared ministry can generate. The call is not a commanding sound. It is the sound of a seed husk opening.

Letting Go of Unilateral Power

Bernard Loomer, a leading process/relational theologian at the University of Chicago Divinity School when I was a student there, was not known as a sentimentalist. This student of Henry Nelson Wieman said bluntly that the basis of human relationship is power, and he worked to develop a more "humanizing conception of power."[1] The usual ways we think about power, he said, are "inadequate for the emergence of individuals and societies of the stature required in today's world."[2]

He said that we usually think about power in one of two ways. What we typically mean by "power" he calls "unilateral power." This is the ability to produce a desired effect on another person, without being influenced in return. If it has a one-way-only effect, it is unilateral power, even if we intend that our effect will be only for the other person's good. Unilateral power is non-mutual relatedness.

A life lived this way, Loomer says, is "religiously inadequate"[3] because it turns the other person, and then even nature and God, into something abstract, remote, and manipulable. Those who live and interact on the basis of unilateral power are "oblivious to the dimension of unfathomable mystery that is present in all our experience."[4] That way of living diminishes people's ability to savor and to respond to the full range of experience because a lifestyle of unilateral power prevents people from relating richly to "the strangeness of life and the hiddenness of its meaning."[5]

Loomer's alternative concept of power represents a major shift in orientation for theology, for human relations, and for other important considerations including ministry, spiritual development, and all aspects of congregational life. It requires a letting go of the urge to have an effect on another without undergoing an effect from the other, a willingness to give oneself over to the transformative possibilities of engagement with others. He names unilateral power's alternative: relational power. This is the ability both to affect others and to be affected. He believes that "the capacity to absorb an influence is as truly a mark of power as the strength involved in exerting an influence."[6]

In order to allow oneself to be influenced by another, one must be secure enough and expansive enough in one's own identity to make room within for something beyond oneself. The other does not then appear as an overpowering threat to our sense of our worth, but expands it; indeed, the very world we perceive, and thus live within, is itself expanded when we make room within ourselves for impact from other people.

> The world of individuals who can be influenced by others without losing their identity or freedom is larger than the world of individuals who fear being influenced. . . . The stature of individuals who can let others exist in their own creative freedom is larger than the size of individuals who insist that others must conform to their own purposes and understandings.[7]

Loomer says this way of interacting—this relationship of mutual influence—is the most valuable of human relationships. In it, influences flow back and forth from one to the other. Gifts are given. Gifts are creatively received, not only from the other, but from oneself as well, because dormant powers within are activated by the relationship and begin to stir. These gifts are incorporated into the receiver's emerging self.

Following in the footsteps of his teacher Henry Nelson Wieman, Loomer is saying that an authentic, engaged relationship is mutually creative of its participants. Mutual relatedness is thus a primary resource for spiritual formation. God is at work then and there, creating the world anew.

My reading of church history suggests that over the centuries the training of clergy has largely emphasized developing the skills needed to exercise unilateral power in relation to others "for their own good." This emphasis has been true of mainstream, evangelical, fundamentalist, and liberal schools alike.

Seminary training and clergy continuing education should reevaluate their attachment to unilateral power and should let go into training that helps develop this different kind of power—thus evoking a leadership of mutuality, a shared and mutual ministry grounded in relational power.

Letting Go into Non-Anxious Leadership

One of my colleagues laughed out loud when I told him the title of this book. He is a good friend and is seldom gentle and often playful in his interactions with me.

"You? Letting go? How ironic!" he laughed.

He is a fine parish minister whom I have known for many years. He's had a long ministry in a healthy parish. He is about as "laid back" as I can imagine an active, effective clergyman being. He seems the epitome of the "non-anxious" leader that Rabbi Edwin Friedman said leaders need to learn to be. And he hasn't studied it; it seems to come to him naturally.

I recognized the wisdom of Friedman's teaching when I first heard about it. I sensed he was a person who could teach me something I wanted to learn about ministry. For a number of years I participated in Friedman's clergy seminars in Maryland. I learned from those sessions that leadership is more about stance than it is about particular actions taken or decisions made. One's *being* is key.

The leader mustn't get into every puzzle, mustn't choose a side in every fray, and mustn't express opinions on every subject. In Friedman's view the leader works to become clear about his or her own beliefs, to differentiate who she is, to be clear with others where he stands, what he intends to do. The challenge is to be clear about one's own position and not to impose one's beliefs on others. That stance is not really aloof, though it may appear so. This isn't about learning to go underground or to blend in. It's just the opposite—but not so as to impose, not to push, not to presume. The well-differentiated leader has an effect on a group like the effect of a magnet passed under iron filings on a piece of cardboard, Friedman said. In the presence of well-differentiated leaders, things line up and find their own position in alignment with the general direction of the group.

Some leaders come naturally to this ability to differentiate. Friedman believed it could be taught. My experience tells me it can be learned—over time, gradually.

Some people who know me well or have worked with me will probably join my colleague in finding irony here, but they couldn't be any more surprised than I was recently when, in a congregation with which I had been consulting, person after person said what a relaxed and easy-going fellow I am. There had been significant intensities in that group and I frequently felt anything but mellow inside. Friedman said a leader is a "non-anxious presence." He didn't say a leader feels no anxiety or runs from the tensions that develop. He said the leader grows spiritually over time in ability to remain present, without getting drawn in. It is possible and necessary to learn how to manage one's anxiety when it arises, as it inevitably will. "Don't just do something! Stand there."

Letting go. Learning to let go. Ironic!

The Poet May Sarton on Letting Go

And now, as the fruit gathers
All the riches of summer
Into its compact world,
I feel richer than ever before,
And breathe a larger air.

I am not ready to die,
But I am learning to trust death
As I have trusted life.
I am moving
Toward a new freedom
Born of detachment,
And a sweeter grace—
Learning to let go.

—May Sarton, from "Gestalt at Sixty"[8]

The Poet Philip Booth on Letting Go

Lie back, daughter, let your head
be tipped back in the cup of my hand.
Gently, and I will hold you. Spread
your arms wide, lie out on the stream
and look high at the gulls. A dead-
man's-float is face down. You will dive
and swim soon enough where this tidewater
ebbs to the sea. Daughter, believe
me, when you tire on the long thrash
to your island, lie up, and survive.
As you float now, where I held you
and let go, remember when fear
cramps your heart what I told you:
lie gently and wide to the light-year
stars, lie back, and the sea will hold you.

—Philip Booth, from "First Lesson"[9]

Chapter 1. From Membership to Ministry

1. Source unknown. The drawing is signed "McPherson."

2. Carl George, *Prepare Your Church for the Future* (Grand Rapids, Mich.: Fleming H. Revell, 1992), 37.

3. Kennon Callahan, *Effective Church Leadership* (San Francisco: Harper & Row, 1990), 106-7.

4. Ibid., 62-64.

5. Ibid., 92-100.

6. Ibid., 101-13.

7. Ibid., 114-23.

8. Ibid., 124-36.

9. John McKnight, *The Careless Society: Community and Its Counterfeits* (New York: Basic Books, 1995), 36-52.

10. Parker J. Palmer, *The Active Life* (San Francisco: HarperCollins Publishers, 1990), 41.

11. Ibid., 43-44.

12. Ibid., 44.

13. Ibid.

14. Martin Luther, *Luther's Works* vol.14 (St. Louis: Concordia Publishing House, 1958), 95.

15. Callahan, *Effective Church Leadership*, 4.

16. Ibid., 3.

17. Peter L. Steinke, *Healthy Congregations: A Systems Approach* (Bethesda, Md.: The Alban Institute, 1996).

18. Loren B. Mead, "Reinventing the Congregation," *Action Information*, (Bethesda, Md.: The Alban Institute, May/June 1990), 2.

Interlude 2

1. Maura Williams, "Not Just on Sunday," *Transforming Liberal Congregations: The Leadership Challenge* 1, no. 2 (summer 1999): 5.

Chapter 2. From Entitlement to Mission

1. Robert Frost, "The Death of the Hired Man," in many collections, e.g., *The Poetry of Robert Frost*, ed. Edward Connery Lathem (New York, Chicago, and San Francisco: Holt Rinehart and Winston, 1969), 34-40.

2. Edward M. Cifelli, ed., *The Collected Poems of John Ciardi* (Fayetteville: University of Arkansas Press, 1997), 221.

3. Walt Whitman, *Song of Myself* (Boston: Shambhala Publications, 1998).

4. Some of the theologians whose writings have influenced my outlook are John Cobb, Michael Cowan, William Dean, Nancy Frankenberry, Gordon Kaufman, Bernard Lee, Bernard Loomer, Bernard Meland, Henry Nelson Wieman, and Daniel Day Williams.

5. John Kretzmann and John McKnight, *Building Communities from the Inside Out: A Path Toward Finding and Mobilizing a Community's Assets* (Chicago: ACTA Publications, 1993), 1.

6. Introduction to "The Capacity Inventory," *Asset-Based Community Development Website*. Northwestern University. July 1999. http://www.nwu.edu/IPR/ciforeward.html

7. Kretzmann and McKnight, *Building Communities*, 5.

8. Ibid., 8.

9. Ibid., 6.

10. John P. Kretzmann, "Building Communities from the Inside Out," *Shelter Force On-Line* (September/October 1995) on the *National Housing Institute Website*. July 1999. http://www.nhi.org/online/issues/83/buildcomm.html

11. Jean Morris Trumbauer, *Sharing the Ministry: A Practical Guide for Transforming Volunteers into Ministers* (Minneapolis: Augsburg Fortress, 1995), tab preceding 25.

12. Ibid., 26.

13. Jean Morris Trumbauer, *Created and Called: Discovering Our Gifts for Abundant Living* (Minneapolis: Augsburg Fortress, 1998).

14. Peter Senge, *The Fifth Discipline: The Art and Practice of the Learning Organization* (New York and London: Doubleday Currency, 1990).

Chapter 3. From Education to Spiritual Development

1. Ralph Waldo Emerson, "The American Scholar," found in many sources, e.g., *Ralph Waldo Emerson: Selected Essays, Lectures, and Poems*, ed. Robert D. Richardson Jr. (New York, Toronto, and London: Bantam Press, 1990), 99.

2. Emerson, "Nature," found in many sources, e.g., Richardson, *Emerson: Selected Essays*, 15.

3. Robert D. Richardson Jr., *Emerson: The Mind on Fire* (Berkeley: University of California Press, 1995).

4. Richardson, *Emerson: Selected Essays*, 4-5.

5. Richardson, *Emerson: Mind on Fire*, 56. (On page 594 Richardson gives

the reference to Henry Scougal, *The Life of God in the Soul of Man*, in Scougal's *Works* (1677; reprint, Boston: Pierce and Williams, 1839).

6. David Robinson, "The Legacy of Channing: Culture as a Religious Category in New England Thought," *Harvard Theological Review* 74, no. 2 (1981): 223.

7. Ibid.

8. Ibid., 228.

9. William Ellery Channing, *The Works of William E. Channing, D. D.* (Boston: American Unitarian Association, 1875), 293.

10. Ibid., 74-75.

11. David Robinson, *Apostle of Culture: Emerson as Preacher and Lecturer* (Philadelphia: University of Pennsylvania Press, 1982), 7-29.

12. Ibid., 12.

13. Robert Cleaver and John Dod, *A Godly Form of Household Government*, 1621.

14. Odell Shepherd, ed., *The Journals of Bronson Alcott* (Boston: Little, Brown, 1938), 105 as quoted in Barry M. Andrews, "The Roots of Unitarian Universalist Spirituality in New England Transcendentalism," *1992 Selected Essays* (Unitarian Universalist Ministers Association, 1992): 23-40.

15. Margaret Fuller, *Memoirs*, as quoted in David Robinson, "Margaret Fuller and the Transcendental Ethos: Women in the Nineteenth Century," *Publications of the Modern Language Association (PMLA)* 97 (January 1982): 85.

16. Michael Quinn Patton, *Utilization-Focused Evaluation: The New Century Text*, 3rd ed. (Thousand Oaks, Calif.; London; and New Delhi: Sage Publications, 1997).

17. See two books by Walter Wink: *The Bible in Human Transformation: Toward a New Paradigm for Biblical Study* (Philadelphia: Fortress, 1973) and *Transforming Bible Study: A Leader's Guide* (New York: Abington, 1980).

18. The eight key themes identifed in the workshop "Our Way of the Spirit" are: The Mystery, The Sacred in the Here and Now, The Divine Seed, Acknowledging the Negative, Variety, Ongoing Revelation, Mutuality, Emergence.

19. The author's Web site is http://www.rdp.cnchost.com

Interlude 4

1. "Storytellers" in "The Talk of the Town," *The New Yorker*, 55, no. 36 (October 22, 1979): 32.

2. Audrey Flack, *Art & Soul: Notes on Creating* (New York and London: Penguin Arkana, 1986), 15.

Chapter 4. From Diversity to Engagement

1. Martin Buber, *I and Thou* (New York: Charles Scribner's Sons, 1960).

2. Lowell Streiker, *The Promise of Buber* (Philadelphia and New York: Lippincott, 1969), 34.

3. Henry Nelson Wieman, *Man's Ultimate Commitment* (Carbondale: Southern Illinois University Press, 1958), 22.

4. Ibid., 23.

5. Ibid.

6. Ibid., 26.

7. Michael Cowan and Bernard J. Lee, *Conversation, Risk and Conversion: The Inner and Public Life of Small Christian Communities* (Maryknoll, N.Y.: Orbis Books, 1997), 88.

8. Michael Cowan, "The Sacred Game of Conversation," *Furrow*, 44 (January 1993): 30.

9. David Tracy, *Plurality and Ambiguity* (San Francisco: Harper & Row, 1987), 19.

10. Cowan and Lee, *Conversation, Risk and Conversion*, 88.

11. Ibid., passim.

12. Judge Learned Hand, *United States v. Associated Press et al.*, District Court, S.D. New York, October 6, 1943 (52 Federal Supplement 362), 372.

13. Ralph Waldo Emerson, *The Journals and Miscellaneous Notebooks of Ralph Waldo Emerson*, vol. 5, ed. William H. Gilman, et al., (Cambridge, Mass.: Harvard University Press, 1960-1982), 177.

14. Parker Palmer, *The Company of Strangers: Christians and the Renewal of America's Public Life* (New York: Crossroad, 1986), 56.

15. John Dominic Crossan, *Jesus: A Revolutionary Biography* (San Francisco: HarperCollins Publishers, 1994), 70.

16. BeFriender Ministry, University of St. Thomas, The Saint Paul Seminary School of Divinity, 2260 Summit Avenue, St. Paul, MN 55105-1094.

17. *BeFriender Ministry Coordinator's Manual* (St. Paul: University of St. Thomas, 1994), sec. 2, 4-5.

18. Michael Cowan, "Emerging in Love" in *Changing Views of the Human Condition*, ed. Paul Pruyser (Macon, Ga.: Mercer University Press, 1987) 66.

19. Dennis Kreuser as quoted in *Transforming Liberal Congregations: The Leadership Challenge*, 1 no. 4 (St. Paul: Unity Church): 5.

20. Peter M. Senge et al., *The Fifth Discipline Fieldbook: Strategies and Tools for Building a Learning Organization* (New York: Doubleday, 1994).

21. Donald A. Schön, *The Reflective Practitioner: How Professionals Think in Action* (San Francisco: Basic Books, 1983).

22. Donald A. Schön, *Educating the Reflective Practitioner: Toward a New Design for Teaching and Learning in the Professions* (San Francisco: Jossey-Bass, 1987).

23. Ibid., 13.

24. Charles Baudelaire, "Intimate Associations," trans. Roy D. Phillips. A slightly different translation of this line can be found in Robert Bly, ed., *News of the*

Universe: Poems of Two-fold Consciousness (San Francisco: Sierra Club Books, 1980), 44.

Interlude 5

1. Bernard Loomer, "Two Kinds of Power," in Bernard J. Lee, *The Future Church of 140 B.C.E.* (New York: Crossroads, 1995), 171.
2. Ibid.
3. Ibid., 179.
4. Ibid., 180.
5. Ibid.
6. Ibid., 184, italics added.
7. Ibid., 185.
8. May Sarton, *A Durable Fire* (New York: W. W. Norton, 1972), 13.
9. Philip Booth, *Relations: Selected Poems 1950-1985* (New York: Viking Penguin, 1986), 4.